TEXTS, TASKS, & TALK

Instruction to Meet the Common
Core in Grades 9–12

BRAD CAWN

Solution Tree | Press

a division of
Solution Tree

555 North Morton Street
Bloomington, IN 47404
800.733.6786 (toll free) / 812.336.7700
FAX: 812.336.7790

email: info@solution-tree.com
solution-tree.com

Visit **go.solution-tree.com/commoncore** to download the reproducibles in this book.

Printed in the United States of America

19   18   17   16   15   1   2   3   4   5

Library of Congress Cataloging-in-Publication Data

Cawn, Brad.
  Texts, tasks, and talk : instruction to meet the common core in grades 9-12 / Brad Cawn.
      pages cm
  Includes bibliographical references and index.
    ISBN 978-1-936763-83-2 (perfect bound) 1. Education, Secondary--Standards--United States. 2. Education, Secondary--Curricula--United States. 3. Common Core State Standards (Education) 4. High school teaching--United States. I. Title.
    LB3060.83.C39 2016
    379.1'580973--dc23
                                                2015031334

Solution Tree
Jeffrey C. Jones, CEO
Edmund M. Ackerman, President

Solution Tree Press
President: Douglas M. Rife
Senior Acquisitions Editor: Amy Rubenstein
Editorial Director: Lesley Bolton
Managing Production Editor: Caroline Weiss
Senior Production Editor: Suzanne Kraszewski
Copy Editor: Rachel Rosolina
Cover and Text Designer: Abigail Bowen

Acknowledgments

Solution Tree Press would like to thank the following reviewers:

Michelle Campbell
Ninth- and Tenth-Grade English Teacher
Elsinore High School
Wildomar, California

Linda Feaman
Literacy Coach and Consultant
Keys to the Core
Glenview, Illinois

Robert Florstedt
English Teacher
Bayside High School
Palm Bay, Florida

Sherri Gould
Literacy Coach
Nokomis Regional High
Newport, Maine

Heather McDonald
English Language Arts Teacher
Denver Secondary School
Denver, Iowa

Esther Wu
English Language Arts Teacher
Mountain View High School
Mountain View, California

Table of Contents

About the Author

Brad Cawn specializes in helping schools and teachers integrate and fully realize the Common Core State Standards for English language arts and literacy across the content areas through rigorous inquiry-based instruction centered on the investigation of disciplinary texts. At the core of this support is an emphasis on the *work* of teaching: professional development that focuses on the design, enactment, and study of instructional practice in school.

Brad serves as an instructor at University of Michigan, where he teaches undergraduate literacy methods coursework in English, social studies, and other content areas; he also teaches graduate coursework in literacy and literacy leadership at Roosevelt University. During 2015 and 2016, he is serving as national director of research on a Gates Foundation–funded project to study exemplary instructional leadership with the Common Core. He has supported some of the largest school districts in the United States, including Los Angeles Unified School District and Chicago Public Schools, and has served as a consultant for numerous U.S. organizations, including the Association for Supervision and Curriculum Development, the Leadership and Learning Center, and the Center for Educational Leadership.

Brad is working on future publications in the area of enhancing academic rigor and the teaching of teaching. He is a pursuing a doctoral degree at University of Michigan, where his research interests include pedagogy of teacher education and the teaching and learning of inquiry-based instruction.

To learn more about Brad's work, visit www.learning-centered.com. Brad also keeps a blog on curriculum instruction, professional development, and teacher education concerns at www.learning-centered.com/blog.

To book Brad Cawn for professional development, contact pd@solution-tree.com.

Introduction

THE NEW STANDARD

The relationship between standards and instruction can often be paper-thin—literally. We've all been there—drawing up a unit or lesson and then dropping the standards on top right before hitting the print button. As high school teachers, we know our students and our content—instruction is surely aligned to standards. But does our instruction address the standards? It's not always clear.

Teaching that is *up to standard* is different. It starts with standards–aligned instructional goals paired to high-quality texts and content. It is learning centered, prioritizing the literacy skills and conceptual knowledge needed for students to be proficient and independent thinkers, readers, and writers in the content area you teach. It is dialogic and inquiry oriented. Student work that is up to standard is different, too: it is *complex*, *knowledgeable*, and *divergent and creative*, to use just a few of the descriptors from the Common Core State Standards (CCSS); it does not fit into a template. This is rigor.

And that, more than anything else in the age of the Common Core, is *the* major shift in both the intention and enactment of teacher practice: teaching, not just text, got complex. There is no program or textbook that provides an easy solution for the challenge of standards; there is no group of instructional strategies—new or otherwise—to readily define what it means to "do" the Common Core or other next-generation standards. The standards, it goes without saying, can't teach themselves.

But wait until you see what's possible with next-generation standards.

New Realities, Possible Futures

At the time of this book's conception, those impacted most by the CCSS—teachers—were hardly on common ground; the ground, in fact, was downright shaky. Surveys reveal a majority of teachers did not like the CCSS (Henderson, Peterson, & West, 2015), were not satisfied with the professional development they had received on implementing them (Education Week Research Center, 2014), and were making few alterations to their teaching to meet new literacy demands (Shanahan & Duffett, 2013). The public and policymakers continue to squabble over the politics of the CCSS. Teachers continue to wonder where the *practice* of the Common Core lies. Often, very little attention is focused on the standards themselves—what they say and what they mean. Given the lack of meaningful, actionable guidance, it isn't surprising that there is even less sustained support to actually enact standards-aligned instruction.

For many of us, then, the question continues to linger: what would it mean to *leverage* next-generation standards in our instruction? Not only should standards inform instruction but instruction should also fully and meaningfully address the standards. We must use what is known about standards to select and synthesize learning objectives. We must also apply strategies of expert practitioners in our fields along with our own knowledge of next-generation assessments (for example, from Smarter Balanced Assessment Consortium [SBAC] and Partnership for Assessment of Readiness for College and Careers [PARCC]) to design authentic, high-quality intellectual work for our students. Essentially, it would mean positioning the standards so they clarify not only what to teach but also *how* to teach it.

For all of the talk of how transformative next-generation standards like the Common Core will be, they are only words on paper until teachers align, apply, and assess expected outcomes in their own practice. Standards matter, of course; but perhaps, more importantly, so, too, do how and why you make them matter. With limited experience teaching with them, and with limited evidence as to what works for teaching to them, shifting practice must focus on *learning* from practice, not simply on accumulating practices.

So, here it is: another Common Core book. This one, though, is different. It is not a book extolling the wonders of the CCSS. (Here's a spoiler: they're good, not great.) It's also not a strategies book. Instead, this book is about the *work* of standards-aligned instruction—the design, delivery, and deepening of teaching that is up to standard. You'll continue to see the phrase *up to standard* throughout this book, and with good reason; it signals that what both teachers and students do—the texts, tasks, and talk—must be worthy of the cognitive rigor of the standards. The measure for change is not magic; it's simply the act of coming to a deep understanding of what students are expected to know and do (your standards), coupled with a deep understanding about what you know as a teacher and what you do as a leader and content expert.

Some may think the Common Core standards are flawed, that they are unclear, questionable, and insufficient. Still, by doubling down on good teaching and deconstructing and rebuilding the standards to support teacher practice, you will see that they support a vision for teaching that is both possible and full of potential. This is why the Common Core is a framework for much of this book's discussion—not merely because it has been widely adopted, albeit not always widely loved, but also because the potential for action is so significant. This isn't a sign that the Common Core should be embraced over and above any other framework, such as state standards or those of an organization. This book embraces teaching *with* standards. Regardless of the standards you use, teaching with them means you are outcome driven, are aligned to the measures students will be assessed on, and have a clear idea of what it means to be proficient in your field at a particular developmental level. So if you're in a state or school that has not adopted the Common Core, when discussion is of specific Common Core language, consider the applications it has for enhancing your own instruction—it is the pattern that matters, not the measure being used.

Much of what it means to do the Common Core—a common expression these days—is a change in perception commensurate with changes in practice. The two are deeply intertwined. To teach ambitiously means to think ambitiously about teaching —about content, curriculum, collaboration, and the capacity of your fellow teachers. What follows is a road map of sorts for a stance to take on your journey toward ambitious teaching *for* learning.

The Core: Teaching for Learning

Ambitious teaching prioritizes the key ideas and problems of a given content area, emphasizes the teaching of critical-thinking skills, and supports all students throughout the learning process (see Lampert & Graziani, 2009; McDonald, Kazemi, & Kavanagh, 2013; Windschitl, Thompson, & Braaten, 2009). Chapter 1 shows how the standards can be applied to enact this kind of instruction. The chapters that follow describe what it means to teach ambitiously in alignment with next-generation standards.

Texts

Content-area instruction that is up to standard starts with consideration of the ways students engage with texts and tasks. What is read, after all, is what is taught, including the content a text addresses, the skills it requires in order to be understood, and the opportunities it offers for students to exchange ideas with one another. Leveraging the text toward strong student engagement entails two key shifts in teacher planning and practice.

1. Selecting texts that are grade appropriate and content rich, and thus worthy of instructional time

2. Providing the right kind of instructional support for students as they are challenged by academic language, abstract ideas, and rigorous tasks related to these texts

You must pay careful attention to both the opportunities and challenges a text provides, what it means to comprehend the specific text in question (and to texts in general—in other words, the standards), and what supports are necessary to ensure students have a complete understanding of the text (Kucan & Palincsar, 2011). A text's complexities should guide instructional decision making about how to teach it. Chapters 2–4 focus on texts.

Tasks

The *task*—what students are actually asked to do with or in response to reading texts—is everything. In combination with the text, it is your opportunity to address and assess multiple standards; it is also the means to craft specific kinds of instructional supports needed to complete the task. Chapter 6 shows how to craft those supports, and chapter 7 looks at the role close reading plays in supporting content-area literacy.

Task construction starts with a meaningful intellectual or interpretive problem—the kind of question or problem that is worth dedicating precious instructional minutes to, requires close reading of multiple texts, and addresses multiple standards. But its most critical component is the way in which instructional time is designed to solve it. This requires you to think deeply about how to train students to read and respond to texts proficiently and independently, develop routines for reading and rereading texts, scaffold through modeling and questioning, and provide meaningful practice and feedback opportunities. This work should not be arbitrarily fitted into four- to six-week-long units; rather, what students are asked to do must dictate the time needed, be it four days or four weeks.

Talk

Finally, we will discuss talk, which chapter 8 explores. In specifying precisely how students should participate with others in reading and understanding texts, the

Common Core college- and career-readiness anchor standard [CCR] one for speaking and listening—"Prepare for and participate effectively in a range of conversations and collaborations with diverse partners, building on others' ideas and expressing their own clearly and expressively"—makes it clear that collaboration and conversation are critical to comprehension (National Governors Association Center for Best Practices [NGA] & Council of Chief State School Officers [CCSSO], 2010). This is *deliberate* talk—it is not student centered for the sake of being more engaging; it is an intentional scaffold to support challenging analytical reading and writing tasks. Student-to-student conversation that is up to standard attends to students' understanding, encourages development of arguments, and seeks to help students build consensus around complex ideas. In other words, it supports collective problem solving with the kind of rich intellectual tasks that should be at the center of content-area teaching.

Collaboration

More than a half decade after the launch of the CCSS, some may argue that there are still no Common Core experts. But expertise, as it has traditionally been defined when a new educational movement arises, is overrated. The kind of expertise needed this time is from within, not from the outside—the kind that derives from actual work with these standards and with your students. It is practice, not expert, based. And it is *shared*. The real work is not in your standards themselves, nor in programs or materials connected to them, but in people and the common ground they share to respond to the challenges and realize the opportunities these reforms create. Teachers, in other words, *make* the difference.

So the best and most critical professional learning on next-generation standards is, in fact, already occurring in your school and in your own classroom—it's what you can learn from your own teaching and your students' learning. Such a practice-based approach puts what you do at the center of what you learn—your experiences as the means for developing your expertise. That's a powerful idea—teacher growth led by classroom practice and by classroom practitioners. The content and focus come out of practice and go back into practice. This reciprocal relationship, with wisdom gleaned from practice then informing the sustained use of wise practices, should be the foundation, the core, of all teacher learning. Chapters 5 and 9 detail mechanisms for building such foundations by illustrating how you and your faculty or colleagues can work together to select and prepare texts for instruction (chapter 5) and study your enactment, including the resulting student learning, of those texts (chapter 9).

Next Steps: Enacting the Standards

Before diving into this book, complete the following two exercises to prime you for the teaching and learning to come.

1. **Read your standards:** Focus on what the standards say *students* should be doing. That's all they're saying: they describe end-of-the year learning outcomes. You may not love them, but what matters is that you understand and align your practice with them. Take, for example, anchor standard four for reading: "Interpret words and phrases as they are used in text, including determining technical, connotative, and figurative meanings, and analyze how specific word choices shape meaning or tone" (NGA & CCSSO, 2010). Undoubtedly, you are building students' word knowledge in your instruction, but are you offering students opportunities to practice grasping how a key word is developed over the course of a text? That's what Reading anchor standard four asks of high school students. Get clear on those expectations, and start thinking about alignment: What can I build on? How can I do it better? Make your starting point *your* teaching.

2. **Read your text:** Locate a passage from a content-area text that inspired or continues to inspire your love for your content—not a text on teaching your content area, but the actual content, such as a poem, a journal article, or a historical analysis. Don't think about the content in terms of your students (yet); think of what challenged or challenges you in the content. For example, think about the last page of *The Great Gatsby* (Fitzgerald, 1925) if you are an English teacher; the first paragraphs of "The Mysteries of Mass" (Kane, 2005) if you are a science teacher; or an excerpt from the introduction of Jared Diamond's *Collapse* (2005) if you are a social studies teacher. Read it again; determine what's important or significant in it. But here's the kicker: write down exactly what you did—the steps, the processes—to understand it. It needn't be an elaborate description, a numbered list of steps will do, but capture every action you took, and record it in the order in which you did it.

Both of these activities will help you familiarize yourself with important information. They show you what it might mean to *enact* the standards. The CCSS were designed to address both content-specific reading concepts (such as sourcing and contextualization in social studies) and more general cross-content literacy skills (such as identifying and using evidence), both of which are necessary to grasp the passage you read in the second activity. You need to teach, support, and assess both.

To do so, you must bring to light what it means to "read and comprehend complex literary and informational texts independently and proficiently" (CCRA.R.10; NGA & CCSSO, 2010) and articulate how it is done. Once it is clear to you what it takes, you'll know how to design instruction for all students in your classroom so that they achieve the same level of understanding.

A Final Note

At many points throughout the text, I refer to evidence in and from the CCSS by way of the anchor standard, the cross-grade and cross-disciplinary literacy expectations for ensuring students are college and career ready, which are notated as CCRA, followed by domain (*R* for Reading, *W* for Writing, *SL* for Speaking and Listening, and *L* for Language) and standard number. Because this book addresses the needs of teachers in multiple subject areas—English, social studies, science, and electives—and across all four grades of high school, use of the anchor standard is merely the general designation that applies to all readers; you should always refer to the corresponding grade-level and content-area standard specific to your teaching assignment to consider how the insight translates into action. Thus, if CCRA.R.2 is discussed, you'll want to turn to, say, RH.9–10.2 if you are a social studies teacher or RST.9–10.2 if you are a science teacher to consider the implications for your classroom; what, in other words, does it specifically articulate about what your students should be doing in terms identifying, tracking, and summarizing key ideas of a text?

FIVE ESSENTIALS TO TEACHING WITH NEXT-GENERATION STANDARDS

The Common Core and other next-generation standards are neither the salvation nor the destruction of education. As standards go, the Common Core and other newer standards frameworks are okay. They are better than most previous standards, to be sure; they are not, however, perfect. But standards don't need to be perfect; they only need to be useful to teacher work—all of the things teachers do to ensure their instruction is up to standard. The Common Core or any other standards framework is, after all, not an initiative; standards are just learning objectives, occasionally vague, and by no means comprehensive. Most importantly, they are nothing without great teaching. The only initiative in the CCSS is what you or others push to do with the standards.

While your literacy standards likely dictate very little about what classroom instruction should look like, they're organized and articulated in ways that, when read closely, provide a framework for what instruction could be. Grab your standards: let's get to work! We will begin by exploring five key ideas for teaching with next-generation standards.

1. Defining daily instruction
2. Reading closely versus close reading

3. Prioritizing critical reading

4. Prioritizing writing

5. Integrating language standards into reading and writing

Remember that the guidance in this chapter is built around the Common Core. If you are not using the CCSS, you can also review your own standards with the following key ideas in mind.

Key Idea 1: Defining Daily Instruction

The first thing to locate in your standards and organize curriculum around are the articulations that address literacy every day in your classroom. In the Common Core, these are Reading standard ten, the text-complexity standard, and Reading standard one, the evidence standard; responding in writing using evidence, Writing standard nine, supports this reading work. Reading anchor standard one invokes both process ("read closely") and product ("determine what the text says"); it identifies both explicit and inferential comprehension as the result of reading, and text evidence as the means by which students demonstrate such comprehension. It also calls for students to have repeated opportunities to read closely to "support conclusions drawn from the text." The kinds of conclusions they draw are encompassed in Reading standards two through nine, which detail the particular kinds of *analysis* and *evaluation* students must do to understand complex texts. Picture, if you will, a ladder: the sides of the ladder are Reading anchor standard one and Reading anchor standard ten, which set the foundation that coursework is based on engaging complex texts, and that students do so by using *evidence* from these texts to demonstrate their comprehension. These sides support the rungs, anchor standards two through nine, which address certain kinds of evidence and uses of evidence in order to demonstrate more sophisticated levels of understanding (NGA & CCSSO, 2010).

The use of the word *analysis* in the grades 9–10 and 11–12 standards of Reading standard one illustrates this ladder relationship: it means students are to regularly engage in identifying evidence, understanding the meaning of that evidence, and using that evidence to explain accounts, processes, concepts, and so on. From this foundation, teachers can then focus on the standards at the highest cognitive level of Bloom's (1956) taxonomy or Webb's Depth of Knowledge (2002):

o Analyzing and strategic thinking (CCRA.R.2–6, CCRA.W.2)

o Evaluating (CCRA.R.8, CCRA.W.1)

o Synthesizing or extended thinking (CCRA.R.7, 9; CCRA.W.7–8)

What are the implications of this structure for instruction? Look to the title of this book, *Texts, Tasks, and Talk*, to help build your instructional ladder. Start with the *text*—grade-appropriate complexity in language and content, with the goal of helping students read proficiently and independently (CCRA.R.10). Concurrently, align *tasks* to help students ascertain and analyze the specific features of the text (CCRA.R.2–9) to literally and inferentially comprehend; finally, use deliberate *talk* to help students articulate this comprehension in discussion (CCRA.SL.1) and writing (CCRA.W.9).

Key Idea 2: Reading Closely Versus Close Reading

The chatter surrounding *close reading*—the intensive multiday study of the language and meaning of a single text—would suggest it is the *de facto* method of implementing the Common Core. But neither the term nor the lesson concept is anywhere in the standards themselves. What the Common Core *does* say, although a bit simplistically, is useful: high school students should "read closely" (CCRA.R.1) and, as stated in the introduction to the CCSS, "comprehend as well as critique"— that is, they should be reading to literally, inferentially, and critically understand the text itself (NGA & CCSSO, 2010).

Reading closely, then, means students are constantly being taught how to engage rich content and then use these methods and the texts to solve content-area problems; it means that multiple ways of integrating, understanding, and applying texts are needed to meet the standards, including but not limited to close reading. In fact, all of the things expected in a close reading—the focus and intensity of looking closely at a text, applying the passage, discussing the content among peers—becomes the essential work of the classroom, not a separate or obligatory task. Learning to read complex content-area texts is the mechanism for, not the supplement to, developing disciplinary literacy. In other words, literally *every day* has to be a close reading day.

Key Idea 3: Prioritizing Critical Reading

While next-generation assessments such as the PARCC and SBAC place significantly greater emphasis on the most cognitively demanding learning standards than did previous state assessments (Herman & Linn, 2014), teachers I observed while researching for this book often told me they were challenged in finding time to effectively address the intertextual analysis (CCRA.R.7, 9), argument evaluation (CCRA.R.8), and research inquiry (CCRA.W.7–8) work so prominent on the new assessments.

So, why not start with the most rigorous anchor standards? In the Common Core, these are the Reading anchor standards under the domain Integration of Knowledge and Ideas and the Writing anchor standards under the domain Research to Build and Present Knowledge. *To integrate* is synonymous with *to synthesize*, and, indeed, in two of these three anchor standards for each strand, students are expected to derive new understanding by comparing multiple treatments of a topic or text. The verb *evaluate*, the most cognitively demanding work in the original Bloom's (1956) taxonomy, appears in two out of the three of these anchor standards in the Integration of Knowledge and Ideas domain. This is true across text type (Literary and Informational) and subject area (ELA, social studies, and science and technical subjects). These standards emphasize formation of "coherent understanding" of essential disciplinary concepts (RH.11–12.9, RST.11–12.9) and "address a question or solve a problem" (RI.11–12.7, RST.11–12.7, RH.11–12.7; NGA & CCSSO, 2010). To do so, students in all high school grades and in all content areas need to make sense of "various accounts of a subject" (RI.9–10.7) or "multiple sources of information" (RI.11–12.7, RH.11–12.7, RST.11–12.7). Nearly every standard for grades 9–10 and 11–12 in this strand asks that students engage in multiple cognitive demands to demonstrate proficiency. The same is also true of Speaking and Listening anchor standards two and three, which involve texts as well (albeit multimodal ones or with the original intention of being seen or heard rather than read).

Traditionally, a teacher might position such learning objectives as the culmination of comprehension work; however, it's best to think of them as a foundation or template for your task design, underlying *all* the work you do in your classroom. To start, your instructional activities should either "address a question or solve a problem" (RI.11–12.7, RH.11–12.7, RST.11–12.7); evaluate the claims, evidence, and reasoning of texts (CCRA.R.8); or compare and synthesize multiple texts as a means of deepening understanding of the key concepts and skills of the content area (R.9; NGA & CCSSO, 2010). Starting with one of these processes not only makes critical thinking primary but also centers the work of your classroom on learning how to read in critical and complex ways, moving away from teaching generic comprehension strategies (such as summarizing) and toward helping students navigate the specific complexities of content-area problems and texts.

Key Idea 4: Prioritizing Writing

Most guidance on teaching writing defaults to organizing instruction by genre, as the Common Core and other next-generation standards are themselves organized. The results are unit plans and curriculum maps in which genres are taught in isolation, as if argumentation, for example, is only to be used in October and April, expository writing in November, narrative in September, and so on. This is an arbitrary and counterintuitive organizing principle, most especially because the common forms of high school writing—the literary analysis essay, the lab report, the document-based question (DBQ)—incorporate both expository and argumentative components. Furthermore, in college and career, students will be asked to solve tasks authentic to the discipline or professional context in which they are situated, not based on genre. Writing standards one through three, which dictate students should compose responses in the three core academic genres (argumentative, expository, and narrative), provide useful guidance on the features and structure of students' written responses, but they do little to clarify the thinking and tasks necessary to produce that writing.

Luckily, there are writing standards that do just that. In the Common Core, the Writing anchor standards in the Research to Build and Present Knowledge domain focus equally on building and presenting knowledge—in other words, understanding and responding to sources. Reading and writing here are deeply intertwined; in fact, the Reading and Writing standards largely demand the same kinds of reading, reflecting, and responding from students. Note the following connections.

- *CCRA.R.7, CCRA.W.7:* Engage texts and research to answer a question (including a self-generated question) or solve a problem.

- *CCRA.R.7, CCRA.R.9, CCRA.W.7, CCRA.W.8:* Synthesize multiple sources on the subject to demonstrate understanding.

- *CCRA.R.8, CCRA.W.8:* Evaluate the evidence and reasoning of texts and sources.

- *All Reading and Writing anchor standards, but especially CCRA.W.9:* Draw on and integrate evidence from texts to support analysis, reflection, and research.

Notice the pattern? Students engage with and incorporate multiple sources. They gather, draw, synthesize, and integrate evidence—whether from a Google search or texts supplied to them—to solve content-area problems. This is precisely what the performance tasks on both the SBAC and PARCC assessments demand of students, and it's exactly the kind of work students should be doing all of the time in class. In fact, chapter 6 (page 77) makes the case that your curriculum should be built around offering students as many opportunities as possible to respond to rich content-area readings and problems—this will maximize your opportunities to teach, practice, and assess the argumentative and expository skills your students need.

Key Idea 5: Integrating Language Standards Into Reading and Writing

In the CCSS ELA, the Language standards are the last strand listed, and it's all too easy to cast them aside—especially if you're a social studies or science teacher—or address them in isolation, seeing them as merely grammar or vocabulary. Don't dismiss them. They need to be integrated into your reading and writing instruction; in fact, several of these standards are critical to reading and writing well. Indeed, the standards must be applied *during* reading and writing if students are to, say, "apply knowledge of language . . . to make effective choices for meaning or style" (CCRA.L.3), "use context . . . as a clue to the meaning of a word or phrase" (L.4.4.A), and "demonstrate understanding of figurative language, word relationships, and nuances" (CCRA.L.5; NGA & CCSSO, 2010).

What the Language standards demand, then, is to be taught in tandem with the Reading or Writing standards they best support. For example:

- Making effective choices for meaning or style in their writing (CCRA.L.3) should be supported as students are developing and organizing their ideas in response to the specific demands—content, audience, format, and so on—of a written task (CCRA.W.4).

- Demonstrating command of written conventions of grammar (CCRA.L.1) and spelling (CCRA.L.2) should be supported as students are preparing to complete or publish their writing (CCRA.W.5).

- Applying an understanding of syntax to the study of complex texts when reading (L.11–12.3) should be supported as students analyze and assess the role of structure and syntax in both literary and informational texts (CCRA.R.5).

- Determining the meaning of academic vocabulary in context (CCRA.L.4, CCRA.L.6) should be supported as students identify and analyze the figurative, connotative, and technical meanings of key words (CCRA.R.4); in fact, CCRA.L.4 and CCRA.L.6 essentially provide the *how* to Reading anchor standard four's *what*.

- Analyzing figurative language (CCRA.L.5) should be supported as students read for craft and structure (CCRA.R.4–6); it is the "missing" literary analysis standard, in that it does not appear in the Reading standards proper but is as vital to understanding the language and ideas of a text as organization (CCRA.R.5) and point of view (CCRA.R.6).

One thing that becomes abundantly clear in this key idea is that Reading standards, and especially any act of reading closely, are incomplete without language benchmarks, which are critical to analyzing the nonliteral and rhetorical components of texts. The Language standards in the Common Core, for instance, fill in missing components of literary analysis (for example, figurative language and syntax), and provide further clarity on how to engage in word study. Indeed, when analyzing and preparing texts for instruction, keep your Language standards side by side with your Reading standards as you determine what is complex in a text and your standards-aligned *teaching points*, those complexities on which you'll focus your instruction.

Prioritizing Standards

Throughout this book, you'll read that the task—what students are asked to do—is *the* most important element. Such an emphasis is not at the expense of the standards; it is *because* of them. You might have noticed, in fact, that, save for some of the Speaking and Listening standards (see chapter 8, page 111), almost all of the Common Core literacy standards were addressed in the previous section. This was possible because each standard or standard cluster was given a purpose; they were not seen as obligations. Certain standards were not prioritized over others; they were not apportioned out across a year. As shown in the previous section, standards are dependent on one another; they are not sequenced, but symbiotic. They need to be organized accordingly.

To see this in action, read *across* the strands of your standards, looking for patterns that cut across the Reading, Writing, Speaking and Listening, *and* Language standards. Do you notice the repetition in language and concept? The standards are linked. No individual standard is emphasized over others; what is emphasized are certain kinds of *skills*. For example, consider the following skills that appear in various standards.

- *Constructing evidence-based arguments:* CCRA.W.1, CCRA.R.1, CCRA.W.9, CCRA.R.7, CCRA.SL.2, and portions of CCRA.W.7 and CCRA.W.8

- *Synthesizing multiple sources:* CCRA.R.7, CCRA.R.9, CCRA.W.7, CCRA.SL.2

- *Evaluating arguments:* CCRA.R.8, CCRA.W.8, CCRA.SL.3

- *Accessing information:* CCRA.W.7, CCRA.W.8, CCRA.L.6

- *Analyzing and applying academic vocabulary:* CCRA.RL.4, CCRA.RI.4, CCRA.L.4, CCRA.L.5, CCRA.L.6

This list represents the core of the intellectual work prioritized by the CCSS ELA: that students ought to be analyzing and arguing about texts, in writing and in discussion, from the very first day of every class. If that's the non-negotiable the standards present, students can't learn Reading anchor standard one or Writing anchor standard one only in August and January. Nor can they experience these standards singularly or in isolation from one another. The priority, in other words, is not so much addressing the standards on any given day, but rather ensuring that students have learning experiences (reading across multiple texts, analyzing and inquiring into content-area issues, and responding formally and informally in writing and speaking) that address the multiple standards. This is the core knowledge in the standards and is precisely what the next-generation assessments such as the PARCC and SBAC do—address more than ten standards in a single task. This is also what you must attend to in the design of your instruction.

It is, then, progression and not prioritization that truly matters. *Prioritization* emphasizes individual standards; *progression*, however, focuses on addressing all or many of the standards and varying the supports—the kinds and complexity of the texts, tasks, and depth of performances—used to assist students. Progression is a necessary mindset when applying the standards because, as an end-of-the-year benchmark, the Common Core can only articulate for you what students should know and do after a year in your class; the responsibility to articulate what that knowing and doing means in September, October, and so on is your own. This progression requires a map of how students might learn the essential skills and knowledge of the standards, a kind of hyper-focused scope and sequence map that could support teaching points and serve as a rubric for students to monitor their progress toward proficiency toward the standards.

Table 1.1 provides a visual representation of such a progression for analyzing and assessing arguments (CCRA.R.8; one of the key critical-thinking benchmarks in the Common Core) and evaluating point of view and reasoning using evidence (CCRA. SL.2; an objective that cuts across all content areas). The example models the grades 9–10 band. Here, the explicit language of the standards serves as the fourth-quarter benchmark. Specifics about the texts analyzed (CCRA.R.10) and the kinds of performances students will complete to demonstrate proficiency (CCRA.W.10, CCRA. SL.4) clarify what it means to succeed independently over time. Teachers deconstruct the standards into individual skills and then backmap these skills across the year so that students continually engage with the standards in ways that increase the quality and complexity of the work in step with their development. At the same time, however, teachers also map out developmentally appropriate performance opportunities with the whole standard to ensure practice opportunities remain complex. Teachers sequence texts, too, so that Lexile complexity, a quantitative measure of the difficulty of the text's language and syntax, increases over the course of the year (1080L–1305L) and that students are exposed to increasingly complex *kinds* of texts. Differentiation can occur in both skill and text, depending on student readiness.

Table 1.1: Sample Learning Progression for Analyzing and Assessing Arguments, Grades 9–10 (RI.9–10.8, SL.9–10.3)

	First Quarter (Q1)	Second Quarter (Q2)	Third Quarter (Q3)	Fourth Quarter (Q4)
Skill articulation: Developing individual skills	Correctly locates the main argument, subclaims, and evidence of a text, including speeches; articulates the stance and point of view of the speaker or writer Takes a personal stance on the efficacy of the text by validating or rejecting specific evidence or key details in the text, as well as by noting any particular stylistic features of the text or speech Identifies and explains false statements	Independently articulates the point of view and stance of the author; can also identify the tone, noting how word choice informs this assessment Maps the argument's claims and evidence; can explain in his or her own words the premises and reasoning or warrant used by the author With support, applies criteria for assessing the relevance and sufficiency of the claims and evidence used	Unpacks specific claims in argument, independently applying criteria to assess the relevance and validity of the reasoning and evidence; identifies and critiques false statements and fallacious reasoning Explains, generally, the connection between point of view and rhetoric, noting how diction, use of evidence, and tone inform the persuasiveness of the text; with support, can analyze usage of rhetorical devices and argumentative techniques in specific passages or paragraphs	Delineates and evaluates the argument and specific claims in a grade-appropriate complex text, assessing whether the reasoning is valid and the evidence is relevant and sufficient; identifies false statements and fallacious reasoning Evaluates a speaker's point of view, reasoning, and use of evidence and rhetoric, assessing the stance, premises, links among ideas, word choice, points of emphasis, and tone
Skill articulation: Developing performance with the standard	By end of Q1, can, with support or with a partner, delineate and evaluate the argument and specific claims in a grade-appropriate complex text, at the lower end of the grade band	By end of Q2, can delineate and evaluate the argument and specific claims in a grade-appropriate complex text, at the lower end of the grade band	By end of Q3, can delineate and evaluate the argument and specific claims in a grade-appropriate complex text, at the middle of the grade band	

continued →

	First Quarter (Q1)	Second Quarter (Q2)	Third Quarter (Q3)	Fourth Quarter (Q4)
Potential work products with corresponding Lexile scores	Editorials or opinion articles, personal essays, speeches (1080L–1200L)	Speeches, debates, longer editorials or opinion articles (1115L–1200L)	Brief excerpts from literary criticism, speeches or debates, longer argumentative essays, nonfiction independent reading (1150L–1250L)	Short excerpts from philosophical texts, short excerpts from literary criticism, longer speeches or tracts, longer argumentative essays, literary fiction independent reading (1200L–1305L)
Assessments	Short responses in which the main idea of the argument is summarized accurately, group or supported formal-argument analysis, short-answer constructed response, quick writes, and exit slips	Outlines or maps of argument, short formal summary of one to two paragraphs on scope and sequence of argument, in-class process writing argument analysis, and exit slips	One-page response in which alternative or counter approaches to the claims, evidence, or reasoning of argument are articulated, explaining how student attends to the strengths and weaknesses of the argument, and a one- to three-paragraph formal evaluation of logic or style of argument	A formal multipage analysis of an argument, attending to both its logic and style

Visit **go.solution-tree.com/commoncore** for a reproducible version of this table.

Because the literacy standards are organized and articulated similarly across the content areas, a progression like the one in table 1.1 can be leveraged by the entire school with minor adaptions—such as changing the text types—to ensure students are getting consistent practice in these skills and performances in all of their course-work. By honing in on specific skill clusters that address multiple standards, teachers remove the need to obsessively unpack or sequence individual standards; rather, by focusing on the most complex and worthy learning skills across the standards —such as argumentative writing—you identify the teaching points that could enhance student learning in all aspects of their literacy.

Next Steps: Creating Learning Progressions

For a learning progression to be useful to instruction, the process of creating it needs to be instructive. For that to occur, three elements are necessary: (1) all educators enacting the learning must be involved, (2) there must be time to fully develop the progressions and then monitor and revise during and after implementation, and (3) there must be a process that leverages the key tools for teaching—the standards, student work, and the texts—for making strategic decisions. Such a process ensures everyone understands the expectations for students and also builds buy-in for actually enacting practice that supports students in achieving the expectations. What's described in the following six steps is a continual process.

Determine Priorities

Using the guidance provided earlier in the chapter, home in on the critical areas students need to master in order to be college and career ready: for example, analyzing ideas and language in texts, synthesizing evidence from multiple sources in order to solve problems, reading grade-level texts independently, and so on. Identify the literacy standards that address this skill area and place these in the Q4 column of your progression—these represent the priorities for the year. (Visit **go.solution-tree /commoncore** for a blank reproducible version of table 1.1.)

Identify Outcomes

Determine the key cumulative behaviors and performances of the skill cluster by articulating what the summative proficiency of this skill should be—for example, an eight- to ten-page research report or engagement with an independent reading text at the high end of the grades 9–10 band for twenty or more minutes. There may be multiple ways of assessment for each cluster. Place these outcomes in the potential work products row.

Note that while Q4 performances are likely to involve formal essays or other longer or larger tasks, that doesn't mean similar kinds of performances can't be assigned in previous quarters. For example, students might still write an argumentative essay during the first semester or throughout the year; the difference would be that the demands and expectations for their performance—for example, the number and complexity of texts to be used, the writing components expected, and so on—would be less.

Define Ambiguous Language

The language in some of the standards is not likely to be practice ready; in other words, it may not be clear what engaging in the behavior or performance looks like in practice, for either your instruction or the student's work. Writing standard one for grades 9–10, for example, has a number of elements in which the descriptors, while generally comprehensible, give us little information about what it would mean to *teach* these skills. To determine what instruction should look like, first work with your colleagues to identify those words or phrases in the standard that need further clarity (see bolded language in figure 1.1).

Standard: W.9–10.1

    a. Introduce **precise claim(s)**, distinguish the claim(s) from alternate or opposing claims, and **create an organization that establishes clear relationships among claim(s), counterclaims, reasons, and evidence**.

    b. Develop claim(s) and counterclaims fairly, supplying evidence for each while **pointing out the strengths and limitations of both in a manner that anticipates the audience's knowledge level and concerns**.

    c. Use words, phrases, and clauses to link the major sections of the text, **create cohesion**, and clarify the relationships between claim(s) and reasons, between reasons and evidence, and between claim(s) and counterclaims.

    d. Establish and maintain a formal style and objective tone while attending to the norms and conventions of the discipline in which they are writing.

    e. Provide a concluding statement or section that **follows from and supports the argument presented**.

Note: The elements that are not practice ready are in bold.

Source for standards: NGA & CCSSO, 2010.

Figure 1.1: Example of non-practice-ready language in the Common Core.

Teacher teams should have a lot of questions about language from this standard: What is a precise claim exactly? What does it mean to create cohesion? How do the standard's requirements compare to the writing students normally produce? What would be needed for all students to be able to achieve proficiency in these skills over time? The answers to these questions go a long way toward recognizing student needs while learning to write and what that learning might look like over time.

Once the potentially confusing language has been identified, the teams come to consensus on the specifics of what proficient student work would look like in this particular area. For example, a *precise claim* is a claim directly addressing a specific literary element and its effects, rather than a list thesis indicating several literary elements. When it's clear what it would mean to perform up to standard in this area, consider the following.

    o How does this performance goal compare to that of a typical performance of your students?

    o What would it mean to learn and practice this skill over time?

    o How might this skill or performance be articulated or taught to students?

Agree on Interim Benchmarks and Expectations

Start with Q1, think about what your students know and can do: what is their starting point, and what, as a result, is yours? Articulate what you think are the essentials of learning in this skill area during the first forty to fifty days of school; write these in the Q1 column of table 1.1 (pages 17–18). To complete the remaining sections of the chart, discuss what you want to teach students thereafter and what you would expect them to be able to do, incrementally, as the school year progresses. As you come to consensus on what it means to demonstrate a partial, developmental, and with-support understanding in the skill area over time, reflect on four considerations: (1) what components students would likely know or be able to do and to what extent, (2) the level of cognitive rigor at which students could complete these components, (3) the kinds of performances or products expected for this level of understanding, and (4) whether students could produce these performances or products independently or with support. Use your answers to compose initial benchmarks for columns Q2 through Q3.

Triangulate With Student Work

Scan portfolios or other collections of student writing over time to determine students' existing competency or likely competency in the skill areas. What do students, on average, seem to know and what are they able to do in this area? Where do they need additional or different kinds of support? Compare your findings to your initial learning progression and adjust the progression to align with anticipated student needs.

Develop an Initial Plan for Assessments, Texts, and Teaching Points

Use the quarterly benchmarks you articulated to conduct initial brainstorming or decision making about what interim assessments in each quarter might look like, which texts are likely to be at the appropriate level of complexity given the point of year and the task, and what skills you'll need to teach to students. Continue to modify and expand these components over time.

While progressions are a useful planning tool prior to or at the outset of the school year, you can also develop them during the year in *response* to student progress. Because many of the skills and concepts to be taught in your selected skill clusters may not have been articulated fully in your team's previous work, your initial progression is not likely to be fully clear or coherent; it gains clarity *as* you teach and assess student learning, using the experience of trying out the elements of the progression to revise and improve the working document. As the document becomes more refined and focused, it can serve as a kind of standards-based reporting tool of student prog-ress, enabling you to monitor and differentiate supports based on students' progress toward proficiency in the selected standards.

SHIFTING TO COMPLEX TEXTS

Text complexity, as the next three chapters make clear, has upped *teaching* complexity. For students to read and understand grade-appropriate complex texts independently and proficiently, high school teachers must be more intentional about selecting *what* students read, more conscious of *when* they expose students to certain texts, and simply better at *how* they help support students' understanding of these texts. Without a shift in teaching commensurate with the new demands for text complexity, it is unlikely that students will be college and career ready in accordance with the new criteria (Williamson, Fitzgerald, & Stenner, 2014). Texts and teaching, in other words, must both be up to standard in order to foster learning capable of meeting these new demands.

The fundamental difference between next-generation standards like the Common Core and previous iterations of state learning benchmarks is the expectation for what and how students read; it is now an actual standard, and students will be tested on it. That standard, Reading anchor standard ten, is the critical outcome of your work during a given year: it represents students' ability to comprehend—"independently and proficiently"—appropriately rigorous texts with the appropriate intellectual rigor. This is at the core of the work, no matter the content area, but it is also a benchmark for daily instruction. What texts you select and how you support students in meeting the demands of the content are what many of the grade-level articulations of Common Core Reading standard ten defines as the "scaffolding as needed" to enable all students to engage in and do work that is up to standard (NGA & CCSSO, 2010).

This is complex work, but the two principles underlying text complexity are themselves quite simple.

1. What you ask students to read must, as often as possible, be at or above what is deemed appropriate for their grade level.

2. Such texts should contain ideas and language that, beyond simply being grade appropriate, both challenge the reader and contribute to his or her intellectual growth.

Good texts are rich in language, enabling students to practice with texts in the respective grade-level text-complexity band. They are also rich in ideas, enabling students to practice learning and applying the knowledge and skills of other reading standards in your framework. By design, such texts push the limits of students' existing comprehension and fluency skills. They require meaningful instruction and learning opportunities for comprehension. They are, then, very deliberate teaching tools, not only for their content but also for the way they may support students' abilities to understand that content.

The Complex Text in High School

What does it mean for a text to be rigorous high school reading? Lexile scores, the measure of a text's sophistication in terms of its vocabulary and sentence structure, give us a starting point to determine rigor: students should enter high school ready to read Martin Luther King Jr.'s (1963) "I Have a Dream" speech (roughly scored at 1070L) and exit at the end of twelfth grade capable of independently reading passages of philosophy, theory, and criticism, such as that of Stephen Jay Gould (science), Jared Diamond (social sciences), and Leslie Fiedler (English), all of which typically score above 1300L. If such a progression appears daunting, consider how dangerous the status quo has been: the typical college-bound senior leaves high school having engaged entirely or predominantly in texts 150–200 Lexile points below the range of readings they are likely to experience in college coursework; that's the equivalent of one to two years of reading exposure they have not experienced! (See the CCSS appendix A [NGA & CCSSO, n.d.a] for a description of how and why that gap came to be.) A critical aim of next-generation standards is to narrow this gap, hence the recommendations to not only increase the level of text complexity in each grade or grade band but also to establish a range so that students experience a coherent progression of complexity *across* grades. Figure 2.1 displays the text-complexity ranges for all grade bands both before (light gray) and after calibration (black) with the Common Core.

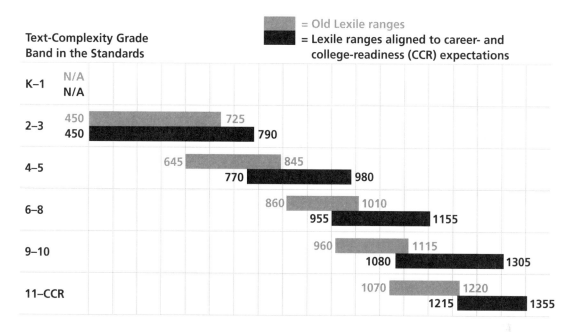

Source: Adapted from NGA & CCSSO, n.d.a.

Figure 2.1: Comparison of old and Common Core–aligned Lexile ranges.

To put it in the most basic terms: high school students need to increase their reading capacity by some 200 Lexile points between grades 9 and 12, and a full 130 Lexile points more than previously expected. In fact, the difference between the old and new expectations for grades 9–10 reading is almost 200 points alone—the low end of the old range is now the high end of fifth grade (Williamson et al., 2014).

Of course, numbers alone only provide a target or a range; they are not sufficient for determining what should be taught. Considered solely for quantitative text complexity, Ralph Ellison's (1952) mid-20th-century masterpiece *Invisible Man* would be classified as a seventh-grade text and the works of Toni Morrison could be taught every year of middle school. What makes high school and college-level texts so complex is in the reading required to understand them, what Jeanne Chall (1983) speaks of as reading for *multiple viewpoints* and to construct a worldview; what William Perry (1999) calls *multiplicity*; and what Mary Field Belenky, Blythe McVicker Clinchy, Nancy Rule Goldberger, and Jill Goldberger Tarule (1997) refer to as *constructed knowledge*. Such readings involve multiple levels of meaning, the use of figurative or rhetorical language, the complex structures meant for a particular purpose or discipline, and so on—they involve not simply the text but the task of reading them closely. The rigor of what students must *do* with the text, obviously, cannot be captured in a quantitative analysis of a text's complexity.

Thankfully, the standards expand on these ideas and provide some guidance. According to the Common Core, complex high school–level literacy experiences in science, English, and social studies involve "multiple sources of information" (RST.11–12.7) or "multiple interpretations" (RL.11–12.7) with "uncertain" (RL.11–12.1), "conflicting" (RST.11–12.9), and "unresolved" (RST.11–12.6) components or implications; possess vocabulary with "figurative, connotative, and technical meanings" (CCRA.R.4); demand analysis and evaluation of the author's premises, claims, and evidence; and include "particularly effective" (RI.11–12.6) uses of language and structure to achieve a purpose (NGA & CCSSO, 2010). At least a third of the Common Core Reading standards in all three subject areas incorporate these components, and the Writing anchor standards and Speaking and Listening anchor standard one do so significantly (NGA & CCSSO, 2010). The word *complex* is repeatedly used to invoke "ideas" (W.9-10.2); "process[es], phenomen[a], or concept[s]" (RST.9-10.2); and the structure of primary sources (RH.9–10.5; NGA & CCSSO, 2010).

As is stated in the introduction to the Common Core State Standards, high school students should be reading to literally and inferentially understand (per the Reading standards) the text itself, but they should also go beyond them to "comprehend as well as critique" (NGA & CCSSO, 2010). Rosenblatt (1994) speaks of the mature reader as engaging in two kinds of reading: *efferent*, reading to understand the content of the text (to learn the *what*), and *aesthetic*, reading to understand the craftsmanship of the writing (to learn the *how*). Note that study of *craftsmanship* is not just for the analysis of literature; it can also refer to precise use of vocabulary or a well-sequenced argument in nonfiction texts, too. That's why all strands in the CCSS have a domain titled Craft and Structure. Teachers should address both efferent and aesthetic reading in all content-area instruction, since they are interwoven, rather than isolated, concepts. For instance, Reading anchor standards one, two, four, five, six, and eight ask students to look at the text while focusing on specific kinds of meaning. Students also must be able to extend their analysis of texts into critical judgments. "Evaluate authors' differing points of view on the same historical event or issue by assessing the authors' claims, reasoning, and evidence" (RH.11–12.6; NGA & CCSSO, 2010), for instance, includes both the understanding of the text (the point of view, the argument) and how it is constructed (assessing the quality of the argument).

Quality, in short, matters. So too does the volume (the amount) and the range (text types) students read, of course, but it is critical that students have plentiful opportunities to read works that display, in the words of the two lead writers of the Common Core ELA standards, "exceptional craft and thought"—and to do so in *all* content areas (Coleman & Pimentel, 2012, p. 5). Social studies and science teachers can't just rely on primary sources or technical documents (such as lab reports); they must also utilize texts that express sophisticated ideas in sophisticated ways—essays, critiques, journalistic pieces, memoirs, and even literary fiction. Students must read for information and to argue and critique, analyze, and aesthetically appreciate language and ideas.

Students have to construct their own meaning *with*, but not necessarily solely *within*, the text. Several of the Common Core standards in each of the content areas make clear that the text assists students in pursuing answers and making decisions. For grades 11–12 social studies, for example, this includes "determin[ing] which explanation best accords with textual evidence" (RH.11–12.3), "evaluat[ing] multiple sources of information . . . to address a question or solve a problem" (RH.11–12.7), and "integrat[ing] information . . . into a coherent understanding of an idea or event" (RH.11–12.9). Thus, a significant purpose for why (and how) students are to engage with complex texts in your content area is to solve meaningful intellectual problems—the same kinds of questions that make professionals read texts closely, such as, "Was the American Revolution really revolutionary?," "Do we need theme?," or "What is the future of the universe?"

This shift is why text complexity has upped teaching complexity: it's not just about putting a more difficult text in front of students—it's about making strategic, deliberate choices about the content you choose and how to ensure students can access it in ways that match the rigor of the standards. For students to comprehend as well as critique, there can't be just one type of text, nor can there be one single way to engender proficient readings; in fact, multiple ways of integrating, understanding, and applying texts are needed to meet the standards.

Further details on the new text and teaching demands for each content area follow.

English

The high school English classroom remains the nexus for extensive fiction and literary nonfiction reading. The amount of literature to include and the focus on analyzing texts have not changed. The difference is that the Common Core State Standards are, in several areas, quite specific about what students should read in English coursework. For grades 9–10, they recommend "a wide reading of world literature" and "seminal U.S. documents of historical and literary significance" (for example, Martin Luther King Jr.'s "Letter From Birmingham Jail"; NGA & CCSSO, 2010). In grades 11–12, they recommend "seventeenth-, eighteenth-, and nineteenth-century foundational U.S. documents of historical and literary significance" (for example, the Constitution), "seminal U.S. texts" involving "application of constitutional principles and use of legal reasoning" (for example, in U.S. Supreme Court majority opinions and dissents), "eighteenth-, nineteenth- and early-twentieth-century foundational works of American literature," and "at least one play by Shakespeare and one play by an American dramatist" (NGA & CCSSO, 2010). The assigning of foundational and seminal nonfiction documents in English is not to remove the responsibility of their teaching from social studies teachers; rather, the idea is for students to analyze and evaluate these works as literature, looking beyond their historical context or importance and at the work itself for, as one standard says, their "themes, purposes, and rhetorical features" (RI.11–12.9; NGA & CCSSO, 2010). This opens up the possibility that students could read the same work in multiple courses, with different purposes for reading in each.

Guidance from PARCC (2012) indicates that students should read at minimum one book-length work per quarter, at least one of which should be nonfiction with the primary purpose to explain or argue. A strong memoir, such as Binyavanga Wainaina's (2011) *One Day I Will Write About This Place*, can supplant a work of literary fiction. Students should read Shakespeare, whose works range between 1200L and 1400L and obviously are qualitatively rich in complexity, at least once in both the lower and upper grades of high school. While English teachers will need to devote at least one of their literary or dramatic works and some of their poetry to classic American literature (such as Nathaniel Hawthorne, Lorraine Hansberry, and T. S. Eliot), the best way to fully address the standards is with contemporary fiction, whose complex accounts and multiple points of view, uncertain resolutions or messages, and intricate characters best reflect the standards. Short story collections from Jhumpa Lahiri (*Interpreter of Maladies*), Daniyal Mueenuddin (*In Other Rooms, Other Wonders*), and Louise Erdrich ("The Red Convertible") can serve as anchor texts, or individual selections can be paired with nonfiction works or used as supplements to other literary works. Finally, students need repeated opportunities to read and respond to five-hundred- to one-thousand-word excerpts from high-quality literary nonfiction (particularly theories, critiques, analyses, and so on, in the areas of aesthetics, the humanities, and sociology), not only to access and experience college-level texts but also because the ACT, PARCC, and SBAC assessments all feature passages of this length.

Social Studies

Social studies teachers have no lack of complex texts from which to choose: most of the seminal and foundational documents of American history identified by the Common Core (such as *Common Sense* and *The Federalist Papers*) are at the high end—if not beyond—the text-complexity range for high school; many of the most well-known and highly regarded historians (such as Jared Diamond and Henry Louis Gates Jr.) are beyond the complexity as well, though more popular writers of society and culture, such as Isabel Wilkerson (*The Warmth of Other Suns*) and Erik Larson (*The Devil in the White City*), tend to fall at the lower and middle ends of the range.

Given the surfeit of quality texts, it is incumbent on social studies teachers to attend to volume and range, offering students repeated opportunities to view both primary and secondary sources of historical phenomena—speeches, essays, autobiographies, visual media, historical fiction, and so on. As with English, social studies teachers should provide many chances for students to read and respond to five-hundred- to one-thousand-word excerpts from secondary sources that reflect the readings students will see on the PARCC, SBAC, and ACT; these should be tied to—or logically connected with—the focus of study at the time of the reading.

Given these demands, it is essential that social studies teachers have a long-term vision for infusing their curriculum with literacy; this requires a consistent structure for how students engage with complex texts in the classroom. Some suggestions:

- Read a book-length text each semester—For example, you could choose to read *The Autobiography of Malcolm X* (Haley, 1965) or a collection of essays, first-hand accounts, and historical analyses of the Civil Rights era. Truly excellent historical fiction, such as Cormac McCarthy's (1985) *Blood Meridian* or E. L. Doctorow's (1975) *Ragtime*, is also appropriate.

- At least once a quarter, if not during each module or unit, include an anchor text that provides a conceptual or theoretical foundation from which students can analyze and evaluate the historical phenomena they are studying—Examples include Arthur Schlesinger's (1986) *The Cycles of American History*, Francis Fukuyama's (1992) *The End of History and the Last Man*, and Jared Diamond's (1997) *Guns, Germs, and Steel*. Students should first study excerpts from such texts so they understand the core tenets of the argument, and then they should apply the key ideas or arguments of the text to examples from the textbook or other readings.

- For each topic or area of study, develop an inquiry by using a balance of primary, secondary, and textbook sources—For example, a U.S. history course could address westward expansion by looking at primary sources of the era, such as John Gast's painting *American Progress* and John O'Sullivan's (1839) "The Great Nation of Futurity" editorial, and secondary sources from a century later, such as Anders Stephanson's (1995) *Manifest Destiny: American Expansion and the Empire of Right*, and Henry Nash Smith's (1970) *Virgin Land: The American West as Symbol and Myth*.

The website Reading Like a Historian from the Stanford History Education Group (http://sheg.stanford.edu/rlh) is a valuable resource for social studies teachers when identifying primary sources.

Science

The challenge for science teachers when selecting and integrating complex texts into their curriculum is addressing the literary side of writing in their discipline. With their technical vocabularies and formal tones, the most common texts of the science classroom—textbooks, lab reports, and technical accounts—are often complex because they are, to borrow a word commonly used by science educators, *dense* with information and technical language rather than because they feature sophisticated arguments, explanations, or uses of language. Teachers need to make a very intentional effort, then, to locate and implement texts that help students analyze, synthesize, and evaluate (per the standards), and not just comprehend; they'll also need to think critically about how to pair *doing* science with *reading* science, as the CCSS do not separate the two.

The following four shifts in science instruction tied to the Common Core standards will help science teachers integrate appropriate texts.

1. **Read and review texts during laboratory exercises:** At least three of the Reading standards for science (RST.9–10.3, RST.9–10.6, and RST.8) specifically address conducting or evaluating procedures and experiments in response to what is written in a text. Others (CCRA.R.7, CCRA.R.9) discuss integrating multiple sources of data, from texts and experiments, into solving problems (NGA & CCSSO, 2010). But simply reviewing a list of steps is not enough—the expectation is that students will read on-level material when engaging in the doing of science, so students will need exposure to the foundational logic of the experiment or question under investigation, such as via the original study (for example, Gregor Mendel's [1865] "Experiments in Plant Hybridization" for an introductory focus on genetics) or the methods section of a scholarly article. Such pieces are also good for addressing vocabulary standards.

2. **Increase the complexity of current event or real-world application articles:** Science teachers commonly share readings that relate to current or recent areas of study. These often are discovered by chance, from not particularly intellectually charged sources, and are utilized in a spur-of-the-moment fashion. Sourcing deliberately from more intellectually rigorous materials, however, is a logical way of helping students use textual evidence (CCRA.R.1) and summarizing complex concepts (CCRA.R.2). The websites of *Science*, *Discover*, and *Seed* magazines all feature articles on the latest science news that are written for the scientific community. Editorial and feature reporting in the *New York Times* or the *Economist* may also suffice. Such works are equivalent to the ideas and rhetorical complexity

of the texts students are likely to see on the PARCC, SBAC, and ACT assessments.

3. **Provide frequent opportunities for students to understand the core questions, arguments, and advances of key scientific concepts:** To integrate complex texts more seamlessly into your curricula, focus reading opportunities on the intellectual development and complexities of key concepts, not on their historical background or practical uses. What makes the writing of scientists like E. O. Wilson, Neil deGrasse Tyson, or Stephen Jay Gould more literary is their inquiry into what is known and unknown in science and their interest in the ethical and philosophical implications of such knowledge. Texts of this quality are particularly good for defining central ideas (CCRA.R.2.), defining technical vocabulary (CCRA.R.4), considering the author's purpose (CCRA.R.5, CCRA.R.6.), and evaluating arguments and explanations (CCRA.R.2). Because such works tend to be rich in thought and intellectually heavy, they need not be long in length. A brief excerpt, sometimes only a paragraph or two, may suffice (NGA & CCSSO, 2010).

4. **Synergize texts:** Reading anchor standards seven and nine ask for students to synthesize information from multiple kinds of texts—prose, visual texts, and quantitative texts—and science teachers can respond by constructing tasks centered on analyzing a range of texts that help students solve a scientific problem (NGA & CCSSO, 2010). For example, in a biology or environmental science class, students might study population decline by reading a theory or technical account of the phenomena and then, using quantitative data and an article on a particular species' decline, identify the cause of the decline, compare it with other species or scientific explanations, and suggest or evaluate solutions. Reading a range of texts— from a complex explanation of theory to a chart to a newspaper article— and engaging in exploration and analysis of data emulates the work scientists do when attacking problems in their field.

Next Steps: Three Implications for Instruction

Looking at the suggestions for all three content areas, it's clear that students need to be reading *authentic texts*—the same kinds of texts professionals in the discipline study and rely on when posing questions and solving problems. They also need to be engaged in *authentic tasks*—the same kind of problems that professionals in the discipline experience or attempt to solve. Rigor, after all, is not just upping the quality and complexity of the content but also equally enhancing the quality and complexity of how teachers and students engage in it. Thus, three implications for instruction are clear: you must (1) ensure text quality is high, (2) ensure reading is a practice, not an act, and (3) make practice deliberate.

Ensure Text Quality Is High

The emphasis on text complexity in the CCSS and talk surrounding the CCSS stem from a report from the testing company ACT (2006), which finds that students' ability to read complex texts independently is the key difference in determining a student's college readiness; at least half of all graduating high school students, the report finds, aren't ready. The big reveal of the report, though, is curricular in nature. The problem is as much one of access as it is outcome: the sophistication and language demands of high school textbooks and student opportunities with and exposure to complex texts in high school have been on the decline for decades.

You've heard the phrase "every teacher a reading teacher"; the Common Core is taking it a step further, suggesting that every *class* is a reading class. In this new reality, the text itself plays a crucial role; more than simply a vehicle for content, a rich text is a vehicle for both teaching the standards and for building student capacity to be proficient and independent readers.

Ensure Reading Is a Practice, Not an Act

The CCSS tell us only what students are to understand; instruction must be the source of *how* they understand. Research tells us that the two essential factors affecting a reader's capacity to understand a text are knowledge and cognitive strategies —that is, what a reader knows about the subject matter, language (including vocabulary), and structure of a text and what the reader undertakes mentally to form a coherent representation of a text, such as by rereading, visualizing, generating questions, and so on (Cain, Oakhill, Barnes, & Bryant, 2001; Liben & Pearson, 2013). These factors work together to help the reader connect language and ideas within the text and across texts or prior knowledge (Magliano, Millis, Ozuru, & McNamara, 2007). If and when comprehension fails, the expert reader has the capacity to monitor and correct as needed in order to establish or reestablish basic comprehension. This ability to grasp the literal and inferential meanings should look familiar—it's Reading anchor standard one, and the student is expected to engage in it during every single class, every single day.

What's radical about these ideas—developing knowledge, utilizing comprehension strategies, building schema, and so on—is that they are hardly radical at all. The research supports them, and the individual pieces are probably already immersed in your school's curriculum, if not your own. But it's no longer only the English teacher who teaches reading strategies, the history teacher who teaches content, and the science teacher who teaches vocabulary. Everyone has to teach everything all of the time. It's a practice, rather than a solitary act. Content, skills, metacognition, and self-efficacy are intertwined and interdependent. A student cannot, say, apply what he or she might have learned about mass in a previous lecture to a *Science* article on the composition of space if he or she is unable to read highly technical scholastic writing; likewise, no set of strategies will be sufficient to understand a primary source account of the French Revolution if a student has no background knowledge on the context, people, or historical significance of the French Revolution. Only through the synthesis of supportive instruction, curriculum, and learning environment can students comprehend complex texts and be ready for the literacy demands of college and career.

Make Practice Deliberate

Selecting texts and attending to the comprehension needs of students is not, however, enough. To ensure student literacy is up to standard, it is crucial to connect intentionally frequent and meaningful experiences with what students are expected to learn—what has been referred to as *deliberate practice* (Ericcson, 2002). The concept, perhaps most widely known as the conceptual basis for Malcolm Gladwell's (2008) 10,000-hour rule for developing expertise, rests on the idea that frequency or repetition of a learned concept or activity alone is not enough to ensure mastery; learners must instead be deliberately engaged in the skill in terms of what they are learning, and when, how, where, and with whom they are learning it. The activity of reading is no different: students must not only be exposed to a variety of texts, they must engage them in a variety of ways—to solve different kinds of problems and to engage others around solving them—if they are to demonstrate increasing independence and proficiency with content that is itself increasing in complexity. The task, not just the text, then, becomes an essential lever for supporting high-quality student work.

The following principles suggest a major shift for educators, particularly when planning instruction. These principals alone are not enough to ensure instruction is up to standard; however, together they provide a foundation for up-to-standard instruction.

- Teachers must develop curricula centered on daily engagement with high-quality texts.
- Teachers must support engagement with high-quality texts through assisted development of comprehension skills, background knowledge, and metacognition.
- Teachers must sequence and scaffold instruction over time so they increase in complexity and autonomy.

Building such a foundation is key to selecting the right texts, aligning standards to literacy pedagogy, and facilitating student engagement with and understanding of rigorous material.

Textbook Supplementation

You'll find no argument here for the elimination of the textbook. By its very nature, however, a textbook alone is insufficient for helping students demonstrate proficiency in the Common Core standards. Mastering a standard requires students to engage with texts rich in thought and language—features a textbook lacks. A student can't analyze where a textbook "leaves matters uncertain" (RL.11–12.1) or "analyze the author's purpose" (RST.11–12.6; NGA & CCSSO, 2010). The Integration of Knowledge and Ideas domain of the Reading anchor standards, requires working with ideas across multiple texts and different kinds of texts, which is something that textbooks, with their discrete chapters and sections, are not set up to do well. Textbooks lack the extended anchor texts students are expected to read in all content areas; many do not feature enough short excerpts of analytical writing that students will need exposure to in order to prepare for the PARCC, SBAC, and ACT assessments. Even if passages used in a textbook are rigorous, reliance on the instructional materials included with the selected text in the teacher's edition of the textbook is likely to be insufficient in helping students demonstrate comprehension that is up to the expectation set by the standards.

Because textbooks provide concise background knowledge and have a neutral tone, there is still a role they can play—provided that role is one of *support* and not presumed to be the learning itself. As part of a text set (see chapter 4, page 53), passages from a textbook can work with a range of other kinds of texts—including visual and quantitative data—to assist students in researching and solving intellectual problems (such as required by Reading anchor standard seven and Writing anchor standards seven through nine). The three-layer technique for including complex texts in social studies coursework—taking a given topic or problem and utilizing a textbook excerpt, a primary source, and a secondary source—can be equally effective in science and English. For example, a science teacher might pair part of a textbook chapter with quantitative data and musings from a contemporary scientist on a given subject. An English teacher might pair textbook language on conducting research with a first-hand account of the research process and an exemplary piece of research writing. In these examples, the textbook *assists* comprehension. It does not provide or result in understanding and application of complex ideas and skill; rather, it supports students in engaging in such work as they read complex texts and complete complex tasks.

CREATING A LONG-TERM VISION FOR COMPLEX TEXTS

Next-generation standards like the Common Core put the text at the center of instructional decision making; it follows, then, that the text should also be at the center of how high school educators prepare to teach. The challenge is that nothing in Reading anchor standard ten, or any standard for that matter, specifically addresses the *how*. The standards, as it is commonly said, address only the *what*. That leaves three lingering questions for teachers to address as they get their curriculum and instruction—and then their students—up to standard.

1. What are the best, most appropriate texts in a given text-complexity band for my students?

2. Because there's a band, or range, of text complexity, how do I structure student experiences with these texts over time?

3. What kind of scaffolding is necessary to ensure proficiency with these texts?

To answer these questions, a teacher needs to deliberately and strategically plan student experiences with texts over both time and skill level, supporting and scaffolding these experiences instructionally. Planning with texts demands the same intensity as planning with standards—that is, it should be a focus all the time. Texts, then, must be a part of the same conversations about standards and intended outcomes—not an afterthought.

This chapter and the next focus on precisely that—mapping out such conversations for both long-term and daily instructional plans. The first two questions—on selecting and sequencing texts—are addressed in this chapter using a *text staircase*. The third question, about how teachers support engagement with the text, is addressed in chapter 4 through discussion of text sets and the various ways a teacher adapts curriculum, instruction, and the learning environment to assist literacy engagement. Texts and teaching, then, are inextricably linked; the end goal is not merely to have more complex texts in schools—it is to develop readers who can comprehend complex texts (Valencia, Wixson, & Pearson, 2014).

A word of caution before beginning the discussion of text mapping: text selection involves more than just the text itself—it involves the *context* as well. The reader, the learning environment, and the task all inform and are informed by the text selection. It's important to keep in mind that the staircase concept described in the remainder of this chapter is not intended for daily (or weekly or unit) instructional decision making; it is meant to prioritize student access to more complex texts over the course of the year.

Building a Text Staircase

Think of a text staircase as a curriculum map for texts—a long-term plan for intentionally exposing students to increasingly complex texts, thereby ensuring students are progressing toward full understanding of the content and skills deemed necessary by the standards across a range of texts. It is a bridge between the standards of a given grade and the content used to teach them, an intentional path to ensure students can move from "with scaffolding as needed" to "independently and proficiently" (CCRA.R.10).

When creating an effective staircase, process matters as much as product: a strong literacy map is the result of collaboration and inquiry. Structure and an outcome-driven approach are also necessary. You want to have rich conversations about rich texts with your colleagues, but you don't want to get lost in the subjectivity of evaluating a text when what's important is the preparation to teach it. That's why the planning process must focus on evidence, particularly on sources of knowledge beyond personal opinion that can support smart decisions about what texts to teach. Data should address multiple components of text complexity (quantitative, qualitative, or reader and task), offer meaningful insight into prospective or established student response to the content (quantitative or qualitative), and encourage rich discussion and consensus building. Possible sources of evidence for building a text staircase include:

- Multiple quantitative measures of complexity (for example, Lexile and ASOS)

- Common Core exemplar texts or PARCC and SBAC samples (qualitative and quantitative)

- Assessment of complexity of text features and meanings (such as text-complexity rubrics)

- Past reading lists or textbooks or those of nearby or comparative schools (qualitative)

- Recommended reading lists (qualitative)

- Reader and task alignment

- Student reading inventories or surveys (reader and task)

- Formative and summative assessment data (reader and task)

What follows is a six-step process for building a text staircase using the example of a grade 9 English language arts team of teachers. Evidence is a critical component, and in several steps of the process relevant data sources are identified to support your thinking. Note that this is not a once-and-done process. You must set aside time to review and discuss texts in relation to the criteria—Lexile ranges, the standards, and so on—as well as to discuss, plan, and implement plans for increasing the complexity of your instruction to meet text-complexity demands.

Step 1: Identify Potential Anchor Texts

The first step is to identify the core, or anchor texts, in a given grade or course that require several days of instruction, book-length fiction and nonfiction work, or denser short texts (such as short stories, essays, articles, and so on) that are worthy of significant instructional time. Teachers in any subject area should have at least one anchor text per quarter. If you are lacking these kinds of texts, you may want to review the examples of possible additions in the ELA standards (NGA & CCSSO, n.d.a) or the exemplar texts in the appendices of the standards (NGA & CCSSO, n.d.a, n.d.b, n.d.c). Potential data sources include current or previous reading lists, recommended reading lists, and Common Core exemplar texts.

The CCSS don't necessarily demand the abandonment of all existing text selections; however, teachers do need to look at the entirety of their literacy plans through the critical lens of whether existing texts support mastery of the Reading standards. Some changes will be necessary, perhaps just supplementation or perhaps replacement. Including more close reading opportunities may mean that your selection of shorter texts will require the most additions or overhaul. Once selected, group the texts according to how they are currently or would be taught—their sequence, the content with which they are associated, and so on.

The teachers on our grade 9 ELA team forego naming the shorter texts initially so they can make those decisions carefully and considerately after determining the touchstones of the course. Their first goal is to make sense of their anchor texts—novels and full works of nonfiction—to see if they meet the Common Core's text-complexity demands. This will help determine how the team will order the texts. Let's presume the course is fairly typical of a grade 9 ELA course. It includes *To Kill a Mockingbird* (Lee, 1960), *The Odyssey* (Homer, 1996), and *Romeo and Juliet* (Shakespeare, 1992)—three of the most commonly taught texts at the freshman level. But at the high school level, some of the Reading standards make more-specific demands on the kind of content to be taught, such as (NGA & CCSSO, 2010).

- Analyze a particular point of view or cultural experience reflected in a work of literature from outside the United States, drawing on a wide reading of world literature (RL.9–10.6).

- Analyze seminal U.S. documents of historical and literary significance . . . including how they address related themes and concepts (RI.9–10.9).

Of course, simply adding a text doesn't ensure the standard will be addressed, but the phrases *wide reading* in the first standard and *documents* in the second tell us that repeated exposure, including anchor texts, will be necessary. While *To Kill a Mockingbird* partially addresses the second standard, and *The Odyssey* partially addresses the first, some additions are in order. To that end, the teachers propose adding Chimamanda Ngozi Adichie's (2003) *Purple Hibiscus*, a coming-of-age story set in 1960s Nigeria, as well as Rebecca Skloot's (2010) *The Immortal Life of Henrietta Lacks*, a nonfiction text on cancer research that has become a popular addition to high school reading lists since its release. The teachers have decided to address shorter texts once they have assessed and sorted these existing and proposed anchor texts.

Step 2: Use Quantitative Measures to Create an Initial Range of Text Complexity

To create an initial sequence of texts based on quantitative scoring, teachers need to use one or more common measures of analysis to see how an individual text compares to established ranges for a given grade. Though insufficient on its own as a text-evaluation tool, the quantitative complexity of a text, which is derived from readability measures like sentence length and complexity, is of use in the text-selection process because of the automaticity and efficiency by which it can be determined. Assigning a numerical value to texts—such as the Lexile score—makes them comparable and enables you to sequence them and distinguish levels of complexity.

The process for considering the quantitative complexity of a text couldn't be simpler: you run your anchor texts through your chosen measure or measures and compare the score of the text against the established grade band range. Table 3.1 shows ranges for five common quantitative measures, each of which has been approved by the Common Core (though Lexile is the default measure by which the writers of the Common Core discuss text complexity). The grade-appropriate range of text complexity is listed for each grade band, 9–10 and 11–12, as well as for the middle school band. While the formulas differ for each measure, all but Lexile use a grade-level equivalent range—that is, the numbers you see listed represent the relative grade level of the text. Thus, as measured by ATOS, grade-appropriate texts for students in grades 9–10 should range in complexity from somewhere between the middle of ninth grade to the end of twelfth grade.

Table 3.1: Approved Measures of Quantitative Text Complexity

Grade Band	CCSS (Lexile)	ATOS	FK	TE	RM
6–8	925–1185	7.00–9.98	6.51–10.34	4.11–10.66	7.04–9.57
9–10	1050–1335	9.67–12.01	8.32–12.12	9.02–13.93	8.41–10.81
11–12	1185–1385	11.20–14.10	10.34–14.2	12.30–14.50	9.57–12

Lexile: Lexile (MetaMetrics); ATOS: Accelerated Reader (Renaissance Learning); FK: Flesch-Kincaid; TE: Text Evaluator (Educational Testing Service); RM: Pearson Reading Maturity Metric (Pearson Education).

Source: Adapted from Achieve the Core, n.d.

The measures in table 3.1 were selected for their accessibility: ATOS, Text Evaluator, and Reading Maturity Metric all have online analysis tools that allow you to upload or paste in text to be analyzed; Flesch-Kincaid is built into Microsoft Word; and Lexile (www.lexile.com) has on its homepage a searchable database of the quantitative measures of thousands of works. A good strategy to employ is to check the Lexile database first to see if the text in question has already been listed; if it has not, which will be the case if the text is not book length (such as with newspaper or journal articles), copy and paste the text into one of the online screeners and see how it compares. This initial finding should then be considered and compared with an analysis via Text Evaluator (Sheehan, Kostin, Napolitano, & Flor, 2014) or Coh-Metrix (Graesser, McNamara, Louwerse, & Cai, 2004), which can assess the topic coherence and complexity of the text's content and determine the aspects of the text most likely to challenge readers (and thus its complexity), respectively.

For our grade 9 example, the teachers ran searches of their proposed titles on the Lexile website and found the results in table 3.2.

Table 3.2: Lexile Scores for the Proposed Anchor Texts

Proposed Anchor Texts	Score
To Kill a Mockingbird (Lee, 1960)	870
Purple Hibiscus (Adichie, 2003)	920
The Odyssey (Homer, 1996)	1050
The Immortal Life of Henrietta Lacks (Skloot, 2010)	1170
Romeo and Juliet (Shakespeare, 1992)	1260

The Lexile range for grades 9–10 in the CCSS is 1070–1305 (NGA & CCSSO, 2010); as you can see, the scores for the proposed anchor texts vary quite a bit, with three in range and two below. There are a few surprises, too: *To Kill a Mockingbird* (Lee, 1960), a staple of freshman year English, is at a fourth-grade reading level. *Romeo and Juliet* (Shakespeare, 1992), commonly taught in the winter of freshman year (and sometimes as early as eighth grade), is at the higher end of the range, more like a text for tenth grade than ninth. RL.9–10.10 and RI.9–10.10 tell us that by the end of freshman year, students should read and comprehend literature and literary nonfiction in the band range proficiently "with scaffolding as needed at the high end of the range," so both *Romeo and Juliet* (Shakespeare, 1992) and *The Immortal Life of Henrietta Lacks* (Skloot, 2010) meet the standard, quantitatively speaking (NGA & CCSSO, 2010); the team of teachers just needs to plan more hands-on supports for the most challenging aspects of the texts.

The teachers have built a staircase where, if they teach the texts in this order, they can say for sure that the complexity will increase over time. But they still have two texts that are not in the 9–10 band range. However, quantitative measures have a long history of underestimating the complexity of literature due to the medium's frequent use of short dialogue and high-frequency vocabulary (such as the repeated use of the word *said*). Thus, making curricular decisions solely based on linguistic complexity also ignores the significant influence the tasks the team assigns have on the reading and the environment in which students learn. So, after looking at the qualitative measures, the team takes a closer look to determine the appropriateness of the proposed texts.

Step 3: Use Qualitative Measures to Determine True Text Complexity

Because quantitative analysis focuses solely on the linguistic and semantic features of texts, it cannot pick up on many of the nuances of a complex text, such as how those linguistic and semantic features are utilized and the meanings they invoke. To show how rich and multilayered the qualities of a complex text can be, the following list shows just a few of the many facets teachers need to consider before rendering a summative judgment on a text (ACT, 2006; Chall, Bissex, Conard, & Harris-Sharples, 1996; Hess & Biggam, 2004; Morsy, Kieffer, & Snow, 2010).

1. Levels of meaning or purpose:

   - How many levels of meaning are there—one level or multiple levels?

   - Is there an explicitly stated purpose or an implicit purpose, which may be hidden or obscured?

2. Structure:

   - Are events presented in chronological order or out of chronological order?

   - Are text traits those of a common genre or subgenre or are traits specific to a particular discipline?

3. Language conventionality and clarity:

   - Is the language literal? Figurative? Ironic?

   - Is the language contemporary and familiar or is it archaic or otherwise unfamiliar?

   - Is the language conversational or is it general academic and domain specific?

4. Knowledge demands:

   - Does the text present common, everyday experiences or clearly fantastical situations, or are they experiences distinctly different from the reader's?

   - Does the text present perspectives like the reader's or perspectives unlike or in opposition to the reader's?

- Does the text require everyday knowledge and familiarity with genre conventions or extensive, perhaps specialized discipline-specific content knowledge?

- Does the text have low intertextuality (few if any references or allusions to other texts) or high intertextuality (many references or allusions to other texts)?

These four categories are the same ones identified in appendix A of the CCSS (NGA & CCSSO, n.d.a). Several states and organizations have developed tools to analyze and assess qualitative text complexity, and all are based on the factors listed here (along with additional factors). For the sake of convenience, this book illustrates teacher conversations using the Text Complexity: Qualitative Measures Rubric (for literature and informational text) created by Student Achievement Partners (Achieve the Core, 2013), which is available online. (Visit **go.solution-tree.com/commoncore** for a link to the rubrics.) Note that because the tools available to teachers may oversimplify thinking about text complexity—inevitable when you reduce the complexities of language to a three- or four-point rubric—intentional conversation about the qualities of text is critical. Complexity derives from teacher thinking and decision making, not a text-complexity assessment tool; it is only through examining how the text is or could be addressed by teachers and students alike that its value can be ascertained.

The primary goal in this step, however, is to further investigate those texts that do not match the text-complexity range and see if they belong in the grade. To do so, review the text against your chosen rubric and discuss both its positives and its constraints. Then, assign a score for each dimension of text complexity from the chosen tool and reach consensus on each text's complexities. This is meant to be a consensus-building discussion; you need to have frank conversations about whether or not the text is sufficiently rich based on established criteria, not personal preference. Once your team addresses the dimensions of qualitative complexity, consider whether the level of complexity identified is sufficient to address the rigor of the standards for the given grade, and if so, *when* it might serve student learning of those standards. Finally, compare the text with similar samples from the appendices of the Common Core (NGA & CCSSO, n.d.b, 2010)—does the text in question show similar conceptual and rhetorical depth?

Let's return to our example of the grade 9 team and consider *To Kill a Mockingbird* (Lee, 1960), which has a quantitative Lexile score that puts it in the fourth- to fifth-grade range. The vocabulary and narrative are, in fact, simple, though complexity is added through the use of dialect and flashbacks. In terms of meaning, there are thematic implications on both an individual level (as a coming-of-age tale) and a societal one (as a tale of morality, justice, and racism), and these are tied to understanding of historical and cultural developments in U.S. society, which is why the Common

Core writers identify it as a grades 9–10 book (and include it in the CCSS appendix B [NGA & CCSSO, n.d.b]). Much of the same is true for *Purple Hibiscus* (Adichie, 2003); while the syntax and vocabulary are quite accessible, the symbolism is complex, and the setting and cultural context require a lot of prior knowledge. It is an early high school text as well. In its descriptive but relatively simple syntax, as well as its use of folkloric and figurative language, it compares favorably to another novel by Nigerian author Chinua Achebe (1959)—*Things Fall Apart*—which is also identified in appendix B of the CCSS as a grades 9–10 book (NGA & CCSSO, n.d.b).

Thus, both texts make sense for novel study during the early part of the school year; the team's initial staircase remains intact, and the teachers will proceed with the same order. Their next step is to enrich the experience by connecting the texts to other complex (but shorter) texts, and to the standards themselves.

Step 4: Identify Supporting Texts

Once you have assessed and preliminarily sequenced the core texts for a class, ensure that these anchors are surrounded and sustained by other rich literacy experiences. While not all of the texts need to be named at this early stage of the instructional planning process, it is important to name at least a few supporting texts that can provide high-quality and varied support to the anchor. These are texts that satisfy both the quantitative and qualitative demands of a given grade band, and they support and connect with what makes the anchor text complex—its genre, content, or themes. It's especially important to select texts from genres different than the anchor (for example, an essay paired with a novel or a newspaper article paired with a lab report).

Complexity, connection, variety—these are the three factors to keep in mind as you select texts. Consider and explore supplemental texts that could meet all three of these criteria for a given anchor. Consider existing texts in the curriculum, but also engage in research and inquiry to see if better options are available. Once you've determined that the quantitative scores of possible supplemental texts are at or above the level of their respective anchor companions, use your qualitative-analysis tool (the Text Complexity: Qualitative Measures Rubric, for example [Achieve the Core, 2013], as mentioned in step 3) to ascertain the components of complexity in the texts by considering how the texts show increasing complexity through or by (but not limited to):

- o **Form or genre**—Provide exposure over time to more difficult or sophisticated kinds of writing (for example, from a book review to criticism, or from a laboratory report to an article in a scientific journal)

- o **Length**—Grow in length relative to form and genre (for example, a longer poem or a longer laboratory report)

- **Content**—Increase in terms of technical, conceptual, or aesthetic sophistication (for example, from atomic particles to the Higgs boson, or from use of cartoons to abstract art)

- **Shades of meaning**—Increase in complexity in terms of the level of abstraction and ambiguity in main ideas and their presentation (for example, use of allegory, satire, and so on)

- **Level of agreement**—Move from affirming the ideas of an anchor text to challenging, critiquing, or deconstructing the content of the anchor (for example, historical analysis of a primary source)

Think developmentally about slotting and timing. For instance, when are students most ready for a particular text and to what extent might the work need scaffolding versus serving as a scaffold for the anchor? Keep the initial focus to about eight to twelve supplemental text decisions so that sequencing is natural and feasible; you can make further decisions about additional texts when designing units.

Recall that our grade 9 team has additional criteria to consider based on the standards: there needs to be a wide reading of world literature (RL.9–10.6) and of "seminal U.S. documents of historical and literary significance" (RI.9–10.9); additionally, the teachers want to increase the amount of high-quality nonfiction, too. These criteria help them focus on a variety of texts—speeches, essays, poetry, memoirs, criticism, and theory—that connect to and extend the anchor texts (see table 3.3).

Table 3.3: Initial Anchor Plus Supplemental Text List

Proposed Anchor Texts	Proposed Supplemental Texts
To Kill a Mockingbird (Lee, 1960; 870L)	Martin Luther King Jr.'s (1963) "I Have a Dream" (1070L)
	Brent Staples's (1986) "Just Walk on By" (1100L)
Purple Hibiscus (Adichie, 2003; 920L)	*Poems* by Christopher Okigbo
	Excerpt from Chinua Achebe's (2009) *The Education of a British-Protected Child* (1150L)
The Odyssey (Homer, 1996; 1050L)	Excerpt from Zachary Mason's (2007) *The Lost Books of the Odyssey* (1200L)
The Immortal Life of Henrietta Lacks (Skloot, 2010; 1170L)	Excerpt from Barbara Lounsberry's (1990) *The Art of Fact* (1300L)
Romeo and Juliet (Shakespeare, 1992; 1260L)	Shakespeare's sonnets 14 and 18
	Excerpt from Erik Erikson's (1968) *Identity: Youth and Crisis* (1300)

Effective supplemental text selection is, essentially, a synthesis of what you know about the anchor text and content, the standards, and your students. *To Kill a Mockingbird*, for instance, offers the team an excellent opportunity to further address the "seminal U.S. documents" demand of RI.9–10.9, as well as to increase the amount of interaction with nonfiction. Martin Luther King Jr.'s (1963) "I Have a Dream" speech and Brent Staples's classic 1986 essay on racism are both accessible in terms of language and content but possess the stylistic and thematic depth to enable close reading. Excerpts from Zachary Mason's (2007) *The Lost Books of the Odyssey*, a revisionist take on Homer's *The Odyssey* that is organized as vignettes from multiple perspectives, address the "shades of meaning" and "level of agreement" criteria described on page 44 by providing a more modernist and less heroic slant on the anchor text. The team decides to position works on psychology (the Erik Erikson [1968] excerpt) and theory and criticism (Barbara Lounsberry's [1990] *The Art of Fact* excerpt) closer to the end of the staircase because of the unfamiliarity of the form and the complexity of the syntax and technical vocabulary, and because they provide unique opportunities for students to reason with and respond to texts in increasingly complex ways.

Step 5: Use the Qualitative Measures to Determine Teaching Points

Identifying what, specifically, is complex about a text can also help you determine exactly what to focus on in instruction. Rather than avoiding or over-scaffolding the challenging aspects of texts, identify a work's points of complexity to designate the areas of need and the necessary instructional supports. Thinking about complexity through the lens of instruction addresses the third component of text complexity: reader and task concerns. Because you know what is complex about the text, you are better able to determine how your students are likely to engage in or struggle with the reading and what you might ask students to do in order to demonstrate whether they are working up to standard.

The focus of this step is to identify the complexity in a text and what, precisely, you and your colleagues will articulate about that complexity. The point at which instruction is most likely necessary is the upper-half of the text-complexity tool you've selected: a *3* or *moderately complex*. The Text Complexity: Qualitative Measures Rubric, for example, moves from use of the word *familiar* to use of the word *unfamiliar* between the *slightly complex* (2) and *moderately complex* ranges. Words like *few*, *easy*, or *familiar* in the descriptors of the text-analysis tool suggest students are able to comprehend the text on their own; words like *implicit*, *abstract*, and *unfamiliar* suggest students need support—guided instruction, close reading, and so on. A *teachable text* is one with enough complexities to be standards worthy but also not so entirely complex as to make it too difficult for students to read independently without significant teacher scaffolding. Record the components of complexity in the Identified Complexity column, as our team of grade 9 teachers has done in the example in figure 3.1 for *Purple Hibiscus* (Adichie, 2003).

Text	Identified Complexity (Based on the Text-Complexity: Qualitative Measures Rubric)	Specific Features of the Text That Are Complex	Standards to Teach
Purple Hibiscus (Adichie, 2003)	*Knowledge demands:* Subject matter is uncommon or unfamiliar to many readers, relying on discipline-specific content knowledge that includes some references or allusions to other texts or ideas.	• African colonialism and postcolonialism • Western versus African religious practices (including allusion of title and biblical allusions) • Use of Igbo language	• "Analyze a particular point of view or cultural experience reflected in a work of literature from outside the United States, drawing on a wide reading of world literature." (RL.9–10.6)
	Meaning or purpose: There are multiple levels of meaning or purpose that are difficult to identify or separate; an implicit, subtle, and complex theme or point is revealed over the entirety of the text in implied, abstract language.	• The parallels between the family's demise and that of Nigeria's • Kambili's identity formation • Purple hibiscus as a symbol	• "Determine a theme or central idea of a text and analyze in detail its development over the course of the text, including how it emerges and is shaped and refined by specific details; provide an objective summary of the text." (RL.9–10.2) • "Analyze how complex characters (e.g., those with multiple or conflicting motivations) develop over the course of a text, interact with other characters, and advance the plot or develop the theme." (RL.9–10.3)

| | *Text structure:* Organization of an expanded range of ideas, events, and plotlines is often implicit or subtle, and may include narrative complexities or discipline-specific material that renders text features useful to understanding content. | • Use of flashbacks for the central narrative, as well as different periods of time for introductory and closing chapters | • "Analyze how an author's choices concerning how to structure a text, order events within it (e.g., parallel plots), and manipulate time (e.g., pacing, flashbacks) create such effects as mystery, tension, or surprise." (RL.9–10.5) |

Reader and Task Considerations	
Reader readiness	Readers' fluency and vocabulary proficiency will need to be at a seventh-grade level or higher, the length of the text may be problematic for some readers, and Igbo terms may be confusing.
Social configuration	We will use primarily small groups, with some strategic use of whole-group (minilesson) and independent (close reading) work.
Assessment	We will use small-group discussion (SL.9–10.1), in-class writing (W.9–10.10), and a summative literary analysis essay (W.9–10.2).
Allocation of time	We have set aside three to four weeks for the novel and unit.
Scaffolding (as needed)	We will introduce background on postcolonial Nigeria (setting). We may need to provide a glossary of Igbo terms for students in advance of reading the novel. We will use minilessons on analyzing character and symbolism development over time.

Conclusion: The novel seems particularly well suited to teaching the Key Ideas and Details and Craft and Structure domains of the Common Core Reading literature standards, particularly as they relate to theme and character and to the standard RL.9–10.6, which requires point of view or cultural experience to be analyzed via world literature; this can justify and support supplemental texts and inquiry into the Igbo culture and the Nigerian political history discussed in the work. A literary analysis essay (W.2) makes the most sense as a summative assessment; formative assessments will likely need to come in ways that engage students and provide daily opportunities to write.

Source: Reader and Task Considerations section adapted from Hiebert, 2012; standards from NGA & CCSSO, 2010.

Figure 3.1: Sample analysis of potential teaching points.

*Visit **go.solution-tree/commoncore** for a reproducible version of this figure and a blank template.*

Once you have recorded the components of complexity, the next step is to name the particular structural, stylistic, modal, and conceptual features that are likely to challenge students, as the grade 9 team did in the Specific Features of the Text That Are Complex column. This work is your bridge from the text back to the standards; these features inform you as to which standards you can use to address or support these complex features—an alignment that facilitates the creation of curriculum maps, units of study, and lesson plans.

The final step is to link the identified complexities of the task to your readers in order to make some preliminary decisions about the contexts and tasks that will compose your instruction. This takes place in the Reader and Task Considerations portion of the figure. There are five considerations to address.

1. **Reader readiness:** What students need to know and be able to do to be ready for the selected text (such as the level of vocabulary or fluency needed, whether experience with the genre is preferred, and affective and personal concerns, including motivation or interest)

2. **Social configuration:** How the classroom and instruction are set up for reading the selected text (such as teacher-led instruction versus independent versus collaborative)

3. **Assessment:** How students will be expected to demonstrate their understanding of what is read (such as writing versus speaking, and formative versus summative assessment)

4. **Allocation of time:** The instructional time necessary to devote to reading and understanding the text (a single period to a whole unit)

5. **Scaffolding:** The supports needed to ensure that students understand the text

Decisions about these elements are meant to be preliminary and based on your knowledge of your students, the learning environment you've created in your classroom, your (and your students') preferred pedagogical approaches, and your instructional plans. Data from assessment programming may also be used here to inform your decision making.

This step uses the Text Complexity: Qualitative Measures Rubric to help make high-level assessments about what is complex. Your knowledge of the text is used to identify the text-specific features of the identified complexities, which are then cross-correlated with specific Common Core standards. (As indicated earlier, only those features of the text rated "moderately complex" or above should be selected as teaching points.) These determinations help you address the reader and task consid-erations, particularly how to assess understanding and provide scaffolds, and make conclusions about how the book might be taught.

Step 6: Put Together the Initial Staircase

Once you select and analyze the initial set of anchor and supplemental texts, the next step is to group them together in a preliminary sequence that connects the texts to the teaching points and reader and task considerations you identified in steps 4 and 5; this work will then serve as a resource for the construction of a curriculum map and subsequent instructional plans.

The key components of this process are gathering the individual text-complexity analyses into a single document and organizing them with the intervals of time most commonly used to organize your school year: quarters, months, units, and so on. As the grade 9 team's work in table 3.4 demonstrates, this level of organization collects all of the important information necessary for formalizing a curriculum: the texts (steps 3 and 4), the standards (step 5), and the initial instructional responses (step 5).

Table 3.4: Initial Staircase for Grade 9 ELA Course

Time Interval	Anchor Text	Supplemental Texts	Primary Standards	Assessment or Task Considerations
Q1	*To Kill a Mockingbird* (Lee, 1960)	• King's (1963) "I Have a Dream" • Staples's (1986) "Just Walk on By"	RL.9–10.1, RL.9–10.2, RL.9–10.4 RI.9–10.1, RI.9–10.2, RI.9–10.4, RI.9–10.9 W.9–10.3	Narrative essay
Q2	*Purple Hibiscus* (Adichie, 2003)	• Poems from Okigbo • Excerpt from Chinua Achebe's (2009) *The Education of a British-Protected Child*	RL.9–10.2, RL.9–10.3, RL.9–10.5, RL.9–10.6 RI.9–10.3, RI.9–10.6 W.9–10.2	Literary analysis essay

continued →

Time Interval	Anchor Text	Supplemental Texts	Primary Standards	Assessment or Task Considerations
Q3	*The Odyssey* (Homer, 1996)	• Excerpt from Mason's (2007) *The Lost Books of the Odyssey* • Excerpt from Vogler's (2007) "A Practical Guide"	RL.9–10.5, RL.9–10.6, RL.9–10.7, RL.9–10.9 RI.9–10.7, RI.9–10.8 W.9–10.1	TBD (Argumentative)
	The Immortal Life of Henrietta Lacks (Skloot, 2010)	• Excerpt from Lounsberry's (1990) *The Art of Fact*	RI.9–10.2, RI.9–10.3, RI.9–10.5, RI.9–10.6, RI.9–10.7 W.9–10.2, W.9–10.7	Research project
Q4	*Romeo and Juliet* (Shakespeare, 1992)	• Shakespeare sonnets 14 and 18 • Excerpt from Erikson's (1968) *Identity: Youth and Crisis*	RL.9–10.3, RL.9–10.4, RL.9–10.7, RL.9–10.9 RI.9–10.3, RI.9–10.4, RI.9–10.5 W.9–10.1	Argumentative essay

In table 3.4, the time intervals are quarters—typical of secondary schools—and the texts are preliminarily assigned to a quarter in the order of their complexity; it need not yet be clear precisely when in the quarter the texts are to be taught, because determinations of module and unit length can be left to curriculum mapping.

Next Steps: Continued Conversation

Developing a year-long map of increasing text complexity, a text staircase, in your course or content area marks the necessary beginning of a fully mapped plan to attend to the standards with your instruction; it is not, however, a comprehensive plan. To develop a comprehensive plan, teachers will need to address the following questions.

- Which standards—particularly those other than reading—are missing or need to be more fully addressed?

- Where are additional texts needed? What kind of texts, and at what level of complexity? (See the next chapter for more on this question.)

- For each anchor text or quarter, how do I sequence and scaffold learning within and across texts? (See chapter 6 for more on this question.)

Continued conversation on what is absent or still needed will help flesh out the remaining curriculum decisions and support standards-aligned instructional decisions; furthermore, it sets up teachers to differentiate additional text selections based on both individual reader profiles and alignment to anchor texts—which are aligned to the standards—thereby addressing all components of the text-complexity process.

PREPARING TEXTS FOR DAILY INSTRUCTION

Whether or not to commit to using more rigorous texts and tasks should not be the question; rather, the question should be *how*—on a given day, in a given unit, given students' current level of capacity and understanding—to do so. Here again is that key planning shift for teachers: the text serves as not only the core of content learning but also the tool by which teachers make determinations for how best to support student learning.

Indeed, in choosing to use a complex primary source or scientific journal article, a teacher's control over what and how to use the text—the purpose, the content focus, the length—is not limited. In fact, preparing texts for teaching is a strategic act of enabling student access. The goal is to leverage the texts—not to mention your ability as an expert reader—as a teaching tool and, conversely, to be proactive about avoiding the potential frustration, disinterest, and distractions that might cause hesitation about increasing complexity in the first place. This chapter discusses two ways of leveraging text as a teaching tool and avoiding potential challenges. The first section discusses how to cluster texts in order to solve rich content-area problems. The second section discusses how to present those texts to students, ensuring access to the ideas students can use to solve the problems.

Clustering Texts for Daily Instruction

Addressing the critical-thinking demands of next-generation standards (such as the Integration of Knowledge and Ideas domain in the CCSS ELA) requires students to read and understand topics, themes, and issues *across* texts. To do so, you need to select and cluster multiple texts to support high-level inquiry, analysis, evaluation, and problem solving. Such a grouping is called a *text set*.

One way to think of the text set is as a kind of instructional curating—a deliberate selecting and positioning of representative texts that can, when leveraged together throughout instruction, extend learning of specific content or background knowledge, assist in the reading of extremely complex or technical language, and provide evidence necessary to formulate arguments in response. For example, a history teacher might use political cartoons and letters from a particular time period paired with excerpts from contemporary historical analyses to help students consider the veracity or validity of an important historical decision. A science teacher might use a chapter from a physics textbook paired with data tables from a related lab experiment and an article from *Popular Science* so students can argue for or against the merits of a scientific phenomenon. These are examples of multiple texts, in multiple forms, leveraged to support the core work of your discipline.

Even if you didn't know the phrase *text set*, you've come to know the idea. The PARCC and SBAC use text sets in their performance-assessment sections. The U.S. history and language advanced placement (AP) exams have included them for years. There is a growing consensus that text sets more effectively position readers to engage texts analytically and critically (Afflerbach & Cho, 2009; Monte-Sano, 2011; Schwarz & Asterhan, 2010). They have been shown to increase content knowledge and the quality of students' interpretations and arguments (Nokes, Dole, & Hacker, 2007; Reisman, 2012; Wiley & Voss, 1999). They demand sense-making processes—comparison and corroboration—unique from and consistently more rigorous than typical reading instruction and activities with a single text or textbook (Litman et al., 2014). They attend to and support both the volume and range demands of text-complexity expectations *and* the critical-thinking components of next-generation standards.

Despite this, regular engagement in analysis and argument from multiple sources during classroom instruction remains quite rare in high school classrooms (Litman et al., 2014). While the structure of the typical high school day and the difficulty of selecting multiple new sources certainly challenge teachers' ability to teach with text sets, the findings suggest the problem is the problems themselves: the tasks students are asked to solve rarely consist of or demand engagement with multiple sources.

Thus, creating and applying text sets must begin with creating and applying the kind of problems that require multiple synergistic texts to solve (Milner & Milner,

2003). However, the number of texts or types of texts in a text set are not what is important; the instructional goals are the priority, and they determine how texts are used and how many—not the other way around (Valencia et al., 2014). The text set is purely the mechanism, the set of tools, to help students solve the problem. It provides the conversation and evidence, but it is what students are asked to do—the task—and what instructional supports are provided that drive student engagement. (See chapter 6 for more on developing intellectual problems.)

When you select texts to invoke students' problem-solving abilities, the focus should not be on volume but rather on *range*—providing students with multiple perspectives or constructions of complex ideas so that they can both comprehend what the texts are conveying and make sense of their implications and significance in light of each piece or the set as a whole. Naturally, comparison matters; you want to select texts that can offer opposing or alternative views, thus providing or encouraging a range of possible perspectives on the problem. But you also want to provide for a range of possible evidence—examples, facts and quantitative data, allusions, descriptive detail and characterization, and so on—that can lead students to make interesting juxtapositions and synthesize new ideas. Attending to range and comparison in the service of solving a challenging intellectual problem will invariably lead to a selection of a diverse set of materials, as the examples of text sets in figure 4.1 (page 56) show.

Notice the variety of text types, including visual texts, in the examples in figure 4.1: they are needed in order to fully and meaningfully answer the guiding problem of the text set. The ideas the texts convey work together to ensure access to complexity, not simply to increase the difficulty of the reading. They also provide significant opportunities to support students in integrating multiple kinds of evidence into their speaking and writing. Notice, too, the frequent use of excerpted texts. Using short samples of sophisticated texts in turn increases access to the kinds of texts that can lead to or support more sophisticated responses: counterarguments, delineations or classifications of ideas, evaluations of underlying values, and so on. Finally, notice that there are no pros-and-cons selections. This is because the problems demand definitions, solutions, and interpretations rather than simple yes-or-no stances; the texts selections, in turn, must provide the content that can help students conceptualize the problem and possible solution, not define it for them. The scope of the problem and the kinds of analysis and argument it demands shape the scope of the text set.

You might have taken a look at the examples and wondered at what level, and how often, you should be developing text sets. The English set, because it incorporates a novel, is clearly at the level of a unit plan, somewhere around three to five weeks of instruction, while the science and social studies examples might be completed in one to two weeks. Units vary in length, of course, but as chapter 6 argues in its suggestion

English: What does it to mean to be an American?
Novel: *Americanah* (Adichie, 2013) or *The Great Gatsby* (Fitzgerald, 1925) Poem: "Won't You Celebrate With Me" (Clifton, 2012) Speech: Excerpts from inaugural addresses by Bill Clinton, George W. Bush, and Barack Obama Essay: "What Does It Mean to Be an 'American'?" (Walzer, 1990) Article: "American Dream, No Illusions; Immigrant Literature Now About More Than Fitting In" (Sachs, 2000)
Science: How should nation-states respond to the challenge of climate change?
Article: "The Physical Science Behind Climate Change" (Collins, Colman, Haywood, Manning, & Mote, 2007) Data table: "Outlooks—Data Snapshots" (www.climate.gov) Report: Excerpt from *Climate Change 2013: The Physical Science Basis* (Intergovernmental Panel on Climate Change, 2013) Report: Excerpts from World Bank's *Turn Down the Heat* (2012) series Article: "A Grand Experiment to Rein in Climate Change" (Barringer, 2012) Report: Excerpt from *Reframing the Problem of Climate Change* (Jaeger, Hasselmann, Leipold, Mangalagiu, & Tabara, 2012)
Social studies: What is the true legacy of the Great Migration?
Nonfiction book: Excerpts from *The Warmth of Other Suns* (Wilkerson, 2010) Primary source: "South Unable to Put Stop to Negro Exodus" (*The Washington Times*, 1916; newspaper article) Historical analysis: Excerpt from *The Southern Diaspora* (Gregory, 2005) Paintings: Jacob Lawrence's Migration series (1940–1941; Lawrence & Bunch, 1993) Fiction: Excerpt from *The Twelve Tribes of Hattie* (Mathis, 2013)

Figure 4.1: Sample text sets.

of an alternative unit of instruction (called modules), units must be built around a key problem and formal response to that problem that incorporates multiple sources; in other words, text sets are needed as often as possible. At the very least, there should be one text set per unit—that is, at least one chunk of at least three instructional periods in which students are examining and responding to multiple texts in order to solve a problem. Ideally, the whole curriculum should be designed around such problems, big and small. The best place to start is by ensuring that opportunity exists for problem solving with complex text sets in the major summative assessments of your course, such as a research project or unit test.

While being well read in your field certainly facilitates the construction process for text sets, the true catalyst for developing many rich text pairings is collaboration with your colleagues on the sorts of intellectual problems that get at the heart of your discipline and drive your instruction. When your team designs problems together, your collective intelligence enables efficient and generative discussion on possible sources to support students' need to problem solve. You can also share in the search process for additional texts in sources or sites where high-quality writing in your field is commonly published (such as the *New York Times*, *Foreign Affairs*, and *Discover*), or even work together to generate a supplemental text, such as a data table.

Use the following questions to guide your brainstorming and development of text sets for your course or grade.

- What texts are needed—and would benefit students—to address the intellectual or interpretive problem fully and meaningfully?

- What texts are appropriate for the grade band and accessible to students at this point in the year or as their reading progresses?

- How would _____ (individual text) contribute to solving the intellectual problem? What aspects of the text are especially useful or meaningful to the problem-solving work? What supports would students need to utilize them?

Start small by going big: reach consensus on the tasks and corresponding text sets that you can use for your major assessments—say a semester final or interim assessment—and then begin to address the performance assessments inside individual courses. Use discussion of potential guiding problems and corresponding texts to direct your decision making.

Presenting Texts in Daily Instruction

This section introduces two methods of strategic preparation of complex texts for student use: (1) excerpting to determine which portions of the text to use and not to use and (2) adapting the text to minimize distractions or focus the text selection.

Excerpting

Perhaps the most logical first move in preparing a complex text for teaching is addition through subtraction: using a part, not the whole, of a complex text. Not all of students' reading opportunities need to be full-length texts; many of their current and future experiences—whether an assigned portion of a chapter or an excerpt on a standardized test—aren't or won't be the full text. It is true that students should be reading more text in general, but what good is assigning a significant amount of text if the ideas in them will only be superficially discussed, if at all? It is better to emphasize a shorter text that students can reread carefully and engage in significantly.

Excerpting is the result of several instructional decisions. The first is matching content to outcome—that is, how the selected text fits and supports the standard or skill teachers are to teach and the key content students are to learn. The second is the role of the text in supporting student learning of the standard or skill—that is, how the learning is structured (whole group versus small group and so on); the instructional approach used to teach the text (such as close reading); and how understanding of the text is to be assessed. It is only then, with these instructional purposes clear, that you determine which parts of the text to use or not use.

As an example, consider Gordon Kane's (2005) "The Mysteries of Mass," a *Scientific American* article on particle physics that serves as an exemplar text for grades 11–12 science in the appendices of the Common Core (NGA & CCSSO, n.d.b). The article is roughly five thousand words (though only about 250 are included in the CCSS documentation), with six illustrations and three sidebars. It contains five different subsections, with topics ranging from a historical overview of science's understanding of mass to contemporary scientists' quest to determine the origin of dark matter. A teacher could choose to focus on the text as a whole or on just parts of it, such as discussion of the Higgs boson. He or she could focus on a particular feature of the text (say an illustration or sidebar), look at several components, or compare it to other texts. There are, in other words, many choices.

There is not, however, an authoritative answer on what's best for students; the only right decision, which you make, is the one reflective of and responsive to the instructional context: the course, the students, the learning environment, and so on. It may be that you teach an AP physics class and assign, in support or in lieu of the textbook, the full article as homework. In a non-AP class, you might instead use classroom time to home in on the theoretical foundations of physics. The focus may be skills driven, such that science teachers look to one of the sidebars or the accompanying illustrations as a way of working on summarizing complex ideas or procedures (as called for by CCRA.R.2), or it may be on conducting a close analytical reading of a longer section so that students can understand technical vocabulary (CCRA.R.4) or how the author structures the text to convey information (CCRA.R.5). Such decision points determine what to excerpt.

It may also be useful to weave together different parts or paragraphs of a text in order to help students concentrate on key concepts and components of the text, while not bogging them down in the technical or scholarly minutiae that often makes teachers reticent to use college-level texts. The text discussed in the next subsection, an excerpt from Norman Finkelstein and Ruth Bettina Birn's (1998) *A Nation on Trial,* was used by a teacher in a world studies class as part of a specific inquiry into whether ordinary German citizens were culpable for the Holocaust (and a general inquiry into whether a community at large can be held responsible for atrocious acts committed by its members). Because the purpose was not to study the Finkelstein and Birn text specifically but to "integrate information from diverse sources . . . into a coherent understanding of an idea or event" (RH.11–12.9), the text—and others like it—were excerpted so that the passages provided expounded on the authors' claims, even if those claims were not always in the same section of text. This gave students an opportunity to read portions of several texts at the high end of the grades 11–12 band while also focusing their reading efforts on solving an instructional task rather than just reading for the sake of reading.

Following are some general rules for excerpting texts.

- If the goal is to examine the text during a day or two of instruction, keep the length to five hundred to fifteen hundred words per excerpt. Not only is this reflective of the length of excerpts on standardized tests, but it is sufficient enough to convey a developed claim and necessary context for that argument.

- The excerpt should have enough discussion and depth to serve as a specific teaching tool for one or more standards: one directly (such that teachers can model and students can practice how to analyze the components of the standard with the text) and one indirectly (such that students can develop ideas, with or without prompting, reflective of what a standard calls for).

- The excerpt should be rich enough to sustain student activity beyond directly addressing the standard or skill. Students should be able to use it to address the intellectual or essential question of the module or unit, connect it to other parts of the same text or different texts, and engage in discussion with one another about its intellectual or aesthetic merits.

- The excerpt should be sufficiently detailed so that minimal frontloading by the teacher is necessary. After all, students are reading the text for a specific purpose, which the excerpt, by design, should help address. The information necessary to understand the work should be in the work.

The reading-to-teach approach discussed in the next chapter is an especially useful process for determining when to excerpt texts and what in them should be excerpted.

Adapting

In some situations, teachers need to go beyond merely selecting parts of text and instead modify or eliminate language that may be superfluous to the instructional purpose of the text, such as the naming of people, events, or concepts that are of little importance to your course of study or the purpose of using content. This avoids overcomplicating the reading process with ideas or language that distract. Adapting is sometimes also necessary when excerpting a text; taking a small section from a larger text may leave references to other parts of the text (or other texts altogether) not contained or fully explained in the excerpt. As Sam Wineburg and Daisy Martin (2009) advise, it's all about focus, simplicity, and presentation—doing what it takes to make the complex accessible to students while maintaining the sophistication of ideas and language of the text.

Let's return to the example of the world history teacher who taught the multiday lesson framed around the intellectual problem "Should the German citizenry be held responsible for the Holocaust?" and featured a range of opinions by scholars on the very subject. Because the instructional objective was for students to evaluate arguments for and against culpability (CCRA.R.8) and then develop and articulate an argument (CCRA.W.1, CCRA.SL.1) in a mock trial, the goal in this particular set of lessons was focused on evidence; the teacher wanted students to grasp and apply the central arguments. He didn't need them, in this case, to parse through an extended careful reading of the scholarship. Therefore, when it came to preparing a text set for students—particularly those who would serve as the judges' tribunal—his goal was to ensure accessibility and application as students worked their way through multiple excerpts from academic sources.

Here, first, is the original paragraph from Finkelstein and Birn's (1998) *A Nation on Trial*:

> With the passage of time and especially as the war took a more disastrous turn, Germans grew increasingly insensitive to Jewish suffering. Propaganda played a part, as did the escalating repression and physical isolation of the Jews. Then the callousness toward human life typically attending war—exacerbated by the terror bombing and worsening deprivations on the home front—set in. Turning ever more inward, Germans focused on the exigencies of survival. Hardened and bitter, in search of a scapegoat, they occasionally lashed out at the weak. To illustrate this gradual coarsening of heart, Bankier first recalls "not unusual" episodes in 1941 when, breaking the law and outraging Nazi authorities, Germans surrendered their streetcar seats to aged Jews, eliciting "the general approval of the other passengers." Yet by 1942, according to Bankier, Germans displaying sympathy for Jews were hooted in public. He recounts a particularly brutal incident also on a streetcar. Citing *only* this last episode in his book, Goldhagen goes on to criticize Bankier's balanced conclusion based on *all* the evidence. (pp. 51–52)

To adapt for the students, the teacher did the following:

With the passage of time and especially as the war took a more disastrous turn, Germans grew increasingly insensitive to Jewish suffering. Propaganda played a part, as did the escalating repression and physical isolation of the Jews. Then the callousness toward human life typically attending war exacerbated by the terror bombing and worsening deprivations on the home front set in. Turning ever more inward, Germans focused on the exigencies of survival. Hardened and bitter, in search of a scapegoat, they occasionally lashed out at the weak. For example, one scholar has written that it was "not unusual" in 1941 to see Germans surrendered their tramcar seats to aged Jews, breaking the law and outraging Nazi authorities but eliciting "the general approval of the other passengers." Yet by 1942 Germans displaying sympathy for Jews were hooted in public.

The most important thing here is what didn't happen: the ideas were not changed, nor were sentences or the structure of the paragraph revised. What was changed, however, were the references to other historians and their ideas that were irrelevant to the purpose of the excerpt and potentially distracting to students' comprehension. Removing direct references to the purpose of the Finkelstein and Birn (1998) text—which was to refute Goldhagen, the historian mentioned at the end of the passage—is not to suggest that the author's purpose isn't important; it simply wasn't important to *this* particular instructional situation, especially when students couldn't refer to the specific texts by Bankier and Goldhagen in question. What *was* important was enabling students to review and discuss multiple perspectives, thus focus was placed on what the students would need in order to identify the central ideas of each article, compare them to one another, and then anticipate the claims and counterclaims of the other groups participating in the mock trial.

It's important to note that the text was not simplified. Rather, the teacher chose what to show and not show the students. It was a deliberate move, one that came out of the teacher's own close reading. Several rereads helped him determine what was important in the text—content-wise and instructionally—so students could do the same.

Indeed, adapting a text requires mirroring what students are expected to do: understand complex ideas, analyze them according to the standards on which the lesson focuses, and apply that understanding to a higher-order thinking task. The only difference is that you also play instructional editor, asking yourself how ideas and language in the text contribute to or distract from what students would do with it. For example, the world history teacher initially considered removing the word *exigencies* from the passage because the word is not commonly used outside of the discussion of rhetoric; however, because the context clues surrounding the word (*survival, focused*, and so on) conveyed its meaning, and because the sentence contributes to the development of the main idea of the passage, the teacher kept it. Furthermore, checking for understanding of the passage by asking two simple questions—"How did ordinary Germans' views change, and why did that change occur?"—also helped the teacher see if students got the gist of the word without having to spend instructional time teaching the word. As it turned out, those two questions were enough for students to understand the author's argument and not need the definition.

This example suggests a three-pronged approach to making adaptation decisions.

1. **Identify challenges:** What, if anything, is likely to frustrate or distract students from achieving the instructional objective of using the text?

2. **Limit over-scaffolding:** Can a careful reading of the text serve to help students understand or get the gist of the word, idea, or background knowledge without teacher guidance?

3. **Project the effect:** How would removing or modifying particular language or ideas in the text affect students' understanding of the passage as a whole? Of the particular sentence or paragraph?

Teachers should make necessary adjustments to help focus student learning on content and the instructional objectives. By enabling continued access to complex ideas, teachers also enable readers to increase their capacity and stamina with rich texts, such that the intensity of the adaption, if any at all, is less and less necessary over time.

Next Steps: Modifying Mindset

If you haven't had a chance to take the reading portion of a high school–level standardized test (say, the ACT) lately, give it a try. You will find it a lot easier than you remember. That's because your knowledge—of the passage content, of the passage text structure, of how standardized testing is organized—enables you to effectively and efficiently respond to the text and problems. Years of systematic instruction and constant exposure to high-quality—or, at least, information-rich—texts gives you this experience and expertise.

Research leaves little doubt that vocabulary and background knowledge are the most significant assets to reading well, but students cannot be well read unless they have the opportunities to read well—repeatedly, skillfully, and meaningfully (Marzano, 2004; Willingham, 2007). That is how you came to be an expert reader; it should be no different for your students, even if it means, as this chapter details, adapting the process. Filling in the background knowledge for them—via lecture, handouts, or simplified sharing of the texts—will not suffice. Students need to be taught how to read complex texts, and they need plentiful practice with what is taught. Teaching will build the background knowledge.

Let's end with what may be the first step in the whole process: modifying mindset. You might have a voice in your head that says, "This is too tough for my students" or "They don't have the background knowledge." You must turn it off. Instead, turn on the voice that says, "How can teaching this text help my students, and how can I help them?" Students need the latter voice. It is the one that not only encourages students engaging in complex texts but also shifts instruction to focus on student learning.

COLLABORATING: READING TO TEACH

For nearly three decades prior to the creation of the Common Core in 2009, the dominant paradigm of literacy instruction focused on what is sometimes referred to as the "just right" book. What students read was determined by what they could read—what was just right for them as determined by the teacher and assessments. When students struggled, what was just right changed: Shakespeare written in contemporary English, a summary of a laboratory report or article rather than the original document, the textbook summary of primary sources, and so on. The text met students where they were.

Those days are over. The new standard is for texts to meet students where they could or should be. In articulating as a standard the reading of grade-appropriate complex texts independently and proficiently, Common Core Reading anchor standard ten makes clear that all students need to have every available opportunity to engage in grade-appropriate complex texts; it is the teacher, not the text, who must now serve as the primary support in enabling student access and understanding of disciplinary content (NGA & CCSSO, 2010).

As detailed throughout this book, the implications and requirements of this shift are significant: more intentional text selection and sequence, more intensive preparation, and more strategic facilitation *during* reading instruction—all facets of professional practice, in other words. To meet these new challenges requires a change not only in what teachers do but *how* they do it, both in their own work and in collaboration with others. Both what it means to be a literacy practitioner *and* a literate practitioner has changed.

The shift starts with recognizing that teaching reading effectively requires educators to be effective readers themselves. Teachers not only must read widely within and across content areas but must also be conscientious of themselves and others as readers—their needs, interests, abilities, and so on. They must read the selected text closely with their students in mind, considering ways to help students comprehend its complexity. To prepare for practice, teachers must also be aware of and apply their own literacy practices to frame the skills and knowledge their students need to access the content (Bain, 2012). If teachers are not close readers themselves, how can they be expected to help students invest the mental, emotional, and social energy necessary to focus for a sustained period of time on words and ideas that may be beyond their initial comprehension? Teaching texts requires teachers to engage in a kind of reading significantly more complex than that of a leisure reader. This *pedagogical reading* must consider students and teaching (Bain, 2012); this is *reading for teaching*.

One way to think about a pedagogical reading is to align your reading for teaching to your standards framework. In other words, your reading considers how the text in question exemplifies certain learning objectives, thereby highlighting those aspects most teachable. Such a tool for English teachers was designed by Chandra Alston and Lisa Barker (2014); an adapted version of it for all content areas is included in figure 5.1.

This pedagogical reading tool is organized by the levels of analysis—meaning, style, and intertextuality—and by the domains of the Common Core Reading and Language standards: Ideas and Details, Craft and Structure, and Integration of Knowledge and Ideas. You can modify the guiding questions for your standards framework, but the underlying principle remains the same: read the text multiple times and on multiple levels to determine what, specifically, is teachable.

Better reading alone, however, is not sufficient. If the new standard for classroom practice is high-quality engagement with complex texts, a new standard is also needed for how teachers design and facilitate student engagement and comprehension of the standards. Such an approach must focus on the text itself—how it is complex, how students might or do interact with it, and how effective pedagogy might support its use. Of course, all teachers *review* the materials they want students to learn beforehand; that is a given. What is suggested here, however, is a different kind of strategy: engaging in the same practices expected of students as a way of defining and refining what and how to teach. After all, if the end game of the Common Core is to have students engage collaboratively and independently in complex texts, demonstrate conceptual and critical understanding of this content, and articulate it powerfully in speaking and writing, shouldn't it follow that teachers ought to prepare for this kind of ambitious teaching just as ambitiously?

	Guiding Questions	**Corresponding Standards***	**Reader Notes**
Meaning	What big ideas, themes, or arguments are articulated by the text?	CCRA.R.2	
Style	What reading strategies (such as questioning and summarizing) are you using as you read to make sense of the text?	CCRA.R.1 CCRA.R.2 CCRA.R.4 CCRA.R.6 CCRA.L.3 CCRA.L.4 CCRA.L.5	
	What aspects of the author's craft are especially evident in this work? Consider: • Genre and structure (narration, point of view) • Rhetorical and figurative language (metaphor, parallelism) • Grammatical and stylistic conventions (passive voice, sentence length)	CCRA.R.4 CCRA.R.5 CCRA.R.6 CCRA.L.1 CCRA.L.3 CCRA.L.5	
Intertextuality	What specific supplementary texts of varying genres (literary and informational) would help students comprehend: • The historical or cultural context of the text or the author's particular perspective • The big ideas of the text • The strategies or craft of the text	CCRA.R.7 CCRA.R.9	

*This figure lists the anchor standards that apply to all content areas and grades; when completing this for texts in your courses, substitute the specific content- and grade-specific standard in the Corresponding Standards column (for example, for a grade 10 biology teacher, CCRA.R.2 would become RST.9–10.2).

Source: Adapted from Alston & Barker, 2014; standards from NGA & CCSSO, 2010.

Figure 5.1: Sample pedagogical reading tool.

*Visit **go.solution-tree/commoncore** for a reproducible version of this figure and a blank template.*

Picture, then, a shared enterprise—you and your role-alike colleagues reading together to teach more effectively. Attending to content, aligning with standards, and anticipating and responding to student needs—all of these things are built into the process of comprehending the text as a teaching tool by:

1. Selecting the text, its purpose, and its alignment to standards

2. Providing opportunities to read and reread the text critically

3. Ensuring consistent understanding and focus among participants

4. Determining what makes the text complex and anticipating student difficulties

5. Attending specifically to teaching the standards that address these complexities

6. Developing the questioning and tasks necessary to help students demonstrate and extend comprehension independently

The next section details how this might look in practice.

Planning a Walkthrough

Suppose we are high school history teachers of a typical junior-year U.S. history course, the kind that broadly surveys the whole of U.S. history. In the past, we have always found ways of including primary sources—such as foundational documents like the *Constitution of the United States* and the *Federalist Papers*—into our work, but with the adoption of the Common Core, our school is pushing us to broaden students' exposure to a wide variety of texts in the social sciences. Because we especially want to support students' work evaluating and developing historical arguments, which three of the nine grades 11–12 history and social studies standards address, we are eager to seek out the kind of secondary sources from key U.S. historians that can serve as models for the kinds of thinking and writing we want our students to do. Because our team agreed to a course organization that subdivides U.S. history into seven time periods—and, therefore, seven units—we built our text staircase (see chapter 3) by picking at least one primary and secondary source for each unit to use for close examinations of argument and text structure. Preparing to teach these new additions guides some of the work of our collaboration unit.

But it is still fall, and we are only just getting into our second unit, the formation of the United States. With the foundational documents of the United States composed during this time, we are not lacking for Common Core–aligned primary sources; however, what we need are texts that express the complexities and challenges that informed these seminal texts of American life, so that students can analyze, evaluate, and argue history. We turn to an excerpt from Gordon Wood's (1992) Pulitzer Prize–winning treatise *The Radicalism of the American Revolution*, considered one of the definitive analyses of the Revolutionary War. The book, at a Lexile of 1280, has a formal but accessible prose style, but also features allusions to other historical events and figures, analyses, and arguments that will be challenging for students; it fits well as a good text for first semester of junior year.

As a reading group, we start first with purpose. We know, of course, that we are only excerpting the text, not reading all of it. For what use, then, is the text to our students' understanding? Even before reading the text ourselves, we consider first why we are doing so; the standards help us clarify what, precisely, that work should be. Because our goal for using secondary sources is to help students assess the validity of historical arguments, we home in on standard RH.11–12.8, "Evaluate an author's premises, claims, and evidence by corroborating or challenging them with other information" (NGA & CCSSO, 2010). Given this goal, and given the premise of the text, we can also formulate a preliminary intellectual problem: just how revolutionary was the Revolutionary War, anyway?

The passage needs to articulate the core of Wood's argument, and must be rich enough for students to be able to draw from other readings they have done in class to corroborate or challenge the argument. Since not all of us have or will have a chance to read the whole book, it makes sense to focus on the general argument as it is presented in the introduction, and then have teachers help students apply that argument to the content and texts already in use in the classroom. We decide to focus on the author's initial set of claims, laid out over roughly three pages.

We choose the following abbreviated excerpt. In preparation for our discussion and preparation to teach, members of the team are asked to come to the next collaboration session having read the selected text on their own and identified areas of the text that are likely to challenge students' comprehension or require focus during classroom instruction.

> Precisely because the impulses to revolution in eighteenth-century America bear little or no resemblance to the impulses that presumably account for modern social protests and revolutions, we have tended to think of the American Revolution as having no social character, as having virtually nothing to do with the society, as having no social causes and no social consequences. . . . For some historians the Revolution seems to be little more than a colonial rebellion or a war for independence. . . . Consequently, we have generally described the Revolution as an unusually conservative affair, concerned almost exclusively with politics and constitutional rights, and, in comparison

with the social radicalism of the other great revolutions of history, hardly a revolution at all. . . .

But if we measure the radicalism by the amount of social change that actually took place—by transformations in the relationships that bound people to each other—then the American Revolution was not conservative at all; on the contrary: it was as radical and as revolutionary as any in history . . . but it was radical and social in a very special eighteenth-century sense. . . . The social distinctions and economic deprivations that we today think of as the consequence of class divisions, business exploitation, or various isms—capitalism, racism, etc.—were in the eighteenth century usually thought to be caused by the abuses of government. Social honors, social distinctions, perquisites of office, business contracts, privileges and monopolies, even excessive property and wealth of various sorts—all social evils and social deprivations—in fact seemed to flow from connections to government, in the end from connections to monarchical authority. So that when Anglo-American radicals talked in what seems to be only political terms—purifying a corrupt constitution, eliminating courtiers, fighting off crown power, and, most important, becoming republicans—they nevertheless had a decidedly social message. . . .

These changes were radical, and they were extensive. To focus, as we are today apt to do, on what the Revolution did not accomplish—highlighting and lamenting its failure to abolish slavery and change fundamentally the lot of women—is to miss the great significance of what it did accomplish; indeed, the Revolution made possible the anti-slavery and women's rights movements of the nineteenth century and in fact all our current egalitarian thinking. . . . The Revolution did not just eliminate monarchy and create republics; it actually reconstituted what Americans meant by public or state power and brought about an entirely new kind of popular politics and a new kind of democratic officeholder. The Revolution not only changed the culture of Americans—making over their art, architecture, and iconography—but even altered their understanding of history, knowledge, and truth. Most important, it made the interests and prosperity of ordinary people—their pursuits of happiness—the goal of society and government . . . In short, the Revolution was the most radical and most far-reaching event in American history. (Wood, 1992, pp. 4–8)

To identify student needs and formulate questions that support understanding, our team starts first by identifying *our* needs and ensuring collective understanding of the text: What argument is the text trying to make? How do we summarize it? Where do we locate the argument, specifically, in the text? As a group, just to ensure we grasp the text, we also identify the gist of the counterargument—again, summarizing and identifying textual evidence—since it is a prominent part of how Wood develops his case. We also take time to offer our preliminary assessments and reactions to the text, giving the group a chance to recognize and appreciate a range of perspectives and responses.

After developing a shared understanding, we start to transition toward understanding the work as a tool for teaching by naming its complex points. Examining a text-complexity rubric (as described in chapter 3), we identify those features that rank as very or exceedingly complex: *organization* and *intertextuality* appear especially complex—the former refers to deep connections between "an extensive range of ideas, processes, or events," and the latter refers to "references or allusions to other texts or outside ideas, theories" (Student Achievement Partners, 2013). While there are other complexities—the syntax in certain parts might rank as very complex —as a group, we are drawn to organization and intertexuality because so much of the author's argument is based on comparing or deconstructing other arguments, including one that distinguishes revolutions by historical period (for example, 18th century versus thereafter). Turning to the text to locate where these complexities lie, and how they correspond with the areas of difficulty and focus we identified during our initial independent reading, right away we see a challenge: someone suggests a distinction between past and modern revolutions, with that distinction defined by social causality. But will students know what *social* means here, and what will they draw from to define it? Already, we are articulating the questioning that will support student understanding and anchor the lesson. One thing we know is that the text itself helps clarify the distinction: How does the social or liberal revolution differ from what the author indicates is the common conception of 18th century or conservative revolutions (for example, intellectual or political differences)? Helping students address this difference will help them follow the argument and evaluate the text.

Moving forward, it should be apparent from the text that the social element is the difference maker in determining the revolutionary quality of a historical event, but we wonder, "Will students grasp the differences in what is considered social in the 18th century versus what it means to the 20th and 21st centuries? The second half of the second paragraph, starting with "Social honors . . . " details grievances about the British monarchy in a way that students may not be familiar with, such that they might not see how a system of patronage causes social ills. As a result, we may need to help students address the question, "What abuses of government compelled the revolution?" and then, "As a result, what does the author mean when he suggests that the political actions of the founders had a 'decidedly social message'?"

In raising these questions, we are not so much suggesting that we take a teacher-led, whole-group-discussion approach to the lesson, or any instructional approach yet, so much as simply trying to understand the text as learner and teacher in a way that we can find our key teaching points. Only then can we think about structure, gradual release, and so on. In this case, our discussion around student concerns and identifying questions to check for and monitor understanding lead us to see that students' initial work of reading the text—as it was for us—must be focused on understanding (1) what distinguishes a social revolution from a more conservative revolution and (2) what argument the author makes about the revolutionary quality of the American Revolution. Aware that these are our initial literal comprehension concerns, we discuss how to address them in instruction: what students should annotate for while reading to help answer these questions, and what sort of visual organizer might help students map out the argument or arguments? We can imagine some of our colleagues will want to focus on comparing the various arguments and some want to focus on breaking down the claims, evidence, and reasoning (CER) of the author, and so discussion ensues until we reach agreement on the best approach to support initial readings.

But that is just attending to a basic comprehension of the reading; it doesn't fully prompt the "evaluating," corroborating," and "challenging" of the argument the selected standard, RH.11–12.8, asks of us. So we reread the text again, focusing on seeing and extending the full measure of the argument. We recognize that, as an excerpt from the introduction of the work, the passage provides us with some meaty reasoning but lacks specifics: the author speaks of a paradigm shift across the social, political, economic, and technological landscape of the United States, but we don't have specific examples here to fully validate. This provides us with an opportunity, however: our students should be able to complete or push back on the argument themselves by selecting and analyzing evidence on their own. The standard requires as much by asking them to evaluate "with other information" (RH.11–12.8; NGA & CCSSO, 2010). Again, we start with our questioning, because that helps us align what we want students to know and do with the standard: What sort of evidence will the author need to validate his argument? Based on what we know about the American Revolution from our studies, what would support the author's claims? What would refute it? We then discuss different kinds of activities to assess learning: Do we want to do a debate? Or a small-group task where students develop the rest of the argument and compare findings with other groups? To ensure total participation of all students, we decide on the latter.

With the initial comprehension exercises and the main collaborative task sketched out, we recognize we have not yet attended to how students independently demonstrate proficiency, so we finalize our initial planning by attending to assessment. We remind ourselves that the standard calls for evaluation, and that constructing a short written argument in response to an idea or text is typically how one responds when evaluating (for example, a review or an opinion essay). We also discuss the need to have students demonstrate this skill in a way that extends, rather than merely repeats, the previous exercises with the passage. As a result, we brainstorm several possible analytic writing prompts that would allow students to spin off new arguments on the text:

- Suppose you were a historian who took the stance that the American Revolution was hardly revolutionary. What claims, evidence, and reasoning would you use to rebut Wood's argument?

- Is Wood justified in suggesting that the revolution was the most impactful event in America's history? Explain, using evidence, why or why not.

- Make a case, using the author's criteria for what qualifies as a radical revolution, for another incident in American history that would also be considered revolutionary.

We decide to each try out one of these prompts with our students to see how the task informs student performance. Our meeting concludes with a member of the group agreeing to write up our findings in the form of a plan for instruction, which the team will continue to revise before we teach the work. We all agree to record observations of student responses and to bring in examples of student work from the independent assessment.

Making Sense of the Walkthrough

This conversation is just one example of one approach to using teaming structures to enhance preparation for literacy instruction. Regardless of the approach, there are several core features that are essential to ensuring both high-quality collaboration time and actionable plans for instruction.

- **Having rich purposeful conversations about text:** Reading and discussing in structured ways serves two significant purposes: (1) it helps build a common understanding on course content and curriculum so that all teachers feel knowledgeable and confident to teach it well, and (2) it helps focus teacher thinking and planning on student understanding from start to finish. Setting goals and rationales—such as identifying the standards to be leveraged through the text—and providing significant time and processes to discuss, problem solve, and plan are necessary to translate the text into teaching.

- **Reading as readers and as teachers:** Just as close reading protocols prioritize multiple readings of the text in order to help deepen understanding and support applications, reading to teach offers multiple opportunities for comprehension: to read as an expert reader, to read as a way of anticipating the challenges of less-expert readers, and to read to teach rigorously. In the past, teachers typically read to plan. The difference here is that teacher reading serves to expand teacher and (likely) student understanding first, so that it then informs planning and doesn't just result haphazardly from it.

- **Focusing on understanding and attending to student challenges or misperceptions:** The shift in onus from the text to teacher in terms of providing scaffolding means educators—all educators—need to be strategic about helping students attack complex texts. The sample walkthrough suggests there is no new or profound approach to doing so; instead, the shift is about mindset, about being strategic in focusing attention on supporting student comprehension, not on strategies. That means taking the time to identify areas of likely difficulty or worthy focus for students, monitoring one's own reading to determine how students might learn to process what they read, and developing questions to help articulate the things students might need to know—or might struggle with knowing—to ensure students sustain comprehension. This focus on comprehension, not simply text selection, prioritizes the interaction among reader, text, and task, better preparing teachers to attend to the demands of the particular instructional situation and context (Goldman & Lee, 2014; Valencia et al., 2014).

- **Ensuring transfer:** Finally, it is essential that students not only demonstrate independent proficiency of the knowledge and skills derived from the text but also apply the experience knowledgeably and skillfully to other learning situations—that is, other texts, other questions, and other tasks. It is not enough, then, to ask students to summarize or explain as a culminating assessment. Instead, teachers must provide new problems to solve and new ways to apply learned concepts. A good text will go a long way toward providing teachers with such application: it will raise and inspire questions, provide many directions within and beyond the text itself, and connect to real-world themes and issues. A collaborating team, then, should deliberately collect and sequence teachers' own questioning about the text—especially in relation to the standards—as a way of determining where students should go with the text, and to help determine how students develop their understanding with and beyond the text.

Next Steps: Planning for Teaching

With your course- or grade-level colleagues, identify a text (or texts) for future instruction that is new to your curriculum; use chapters 3–4 to guide your selection and adaptation of this content. Once selected, read the text together, focusing first on content: what stands out to you and your colleagues as readers, what's worth discussing, what challenged you? Consider the value and implications of these ideas for teaching the text by discussing the following questions.

- Which Common Core Reading standards appear particularly well suited to this text?

- What is particularly complex about the text? Where in the text are students likely to be most challenged?

- What is particularly rich about the text? Where in the text would students encounter this richness?

- What tasks would best support their understanding of the complexity and richness of the text?

Conversation around these questions will pivot into discussing what students need to comprehend the text, and how you can support this comprehension with questions and activities. Use these ideas to formulate an outline of a plan for teaching the text, including how students will demonstrate their understanding of what the text means—or how to read a text for that kind of meaning—on their own.

CREATING
RIGOROUS TASKS

Changes in teaching brought forth by next-generation standards are necessary if students are to master the increasing demands to comprehend and critique complex content. Next-generation standards like the CCSS have done more than simply raise the complexity of texts—they've called for reading, writing, and thinking skills that go beyond traditional definitions of comprehension and therefore go beyond what is typically included in curriculum, instruction, and assessment practices (Goldman & Lee, 2014). Thus, significant adaptation of instruction is likely for many teachers. They will have to carefully and concurrently select and design tasks and texts, provide strategic discipline-specific skills instruction, and increase deliberate opportunities to practice complex thinking and reasoning processes with complex texts (Goldman & Lee, 2014; Williamson et al., 2014). This is no easy task.

Enactment starts with a clear vision about what it would look like to be up to standard—that is, the task and expectations for student performance. Begin, then, with the end in mind: the writing components of the assessments that will define students' college-readiness (such as SBAC), college entry (such as the ACT), or college credit (such as AP). With the Common Core in hand, examine examples of the college-readiness or entrance assessments your students take, first by considering each task individually: what does it demand of students, and how is this different from previous iterations of the assessment, or from other similar assessments? Next, look across the tasks. What seems to be the trend, the connection, in the design and demands of the next-generation assessments?

When engaging in this analysis, you might have noticed that the assessments address and involve many, many standards—the performance assessment on the SBAC alone covers at least ten Common Core standards across Reading, Writing, and Language strands (CCRA.R.1, CCRA.R.2, CCRA.R.7, CCRA.R.8, and CCRA.R.10; CCRA.W.1, CCRA.W.4–.6; parts of CCRA.W.7–9; CCRA.L.2, CCRA.L.3; NGA & CCSSO, 2010). The task type on the performance assessment component of every single college-readiness or entrance examination is argumentative, prompting students to take a stance through analysis and evaluation, use of varied and sufficient evidence, and acknowledgment of multiple perspectives on the issue; all tasks require students to utilize and integrate multiple sources to support arguments. In a word, this is *synthesis*.

Synthesis, considered the cognitive process with the highest level of rigor (Webb, 2002), involves the generating of new claims and conclusions from analysis and evaluation of multiple sources of existing knowledge. Often, such tasks require students to transfer knowledge or skills into new domains or applications. A quick scan of the Common Core reveals that elements of synthesis cut across multiple standards: evaluation of arguments (CCRA.R.8, CCRA.W.8, CCRA.SL.3), accessing and assessing information (CCRA.W.7, CCRA.W.8, CCRA.L.6), integrating multiple sources (CCRA.R.1, CCRA.R.7, CCRA.R.9, CCRA.W.7, CCRA.SL.2), and writing arguments from and with those sources (CCRA.W.1, CCRA.W.2, CCRA.W.8, CCRA.W.9, CCRA.SL.2; NGO & CCSSO, 2010). While synthesis is never explicitly called out in the Common Core standards, the SBAC and PARCC performance assessments make clear that it is the ultimate outcome of proficiency across standards; *college and career ready*, in other words, means being able to synthesize.

If synthesis is the ultimate goal of student learning, and if what students are tasked to do is the basis of their learning, it follows that synthesis tasks ought to be the core of high school-content-literacy instruction (Doyle, 1988). So let's talk *task*. The word is used here to connote in literacy the classroom activity that is devoted to development of a particular content-area idea or skill (see Stein and Smith [1998] for a discussion of the term's use in mathematics), but much more is at stake. Tasks are, yes, what students do or solve—the work of the classroom. They involve a question or problem, the instructional supports to help solve it, the activities and time, and the assessment to measure understanding—the *whole* of the work. A high-quality task amounts to the *doing* of the discipline—the evaluation, the analysis—through rich texts, for a specific skill or content goal, and with a clear idea of the instructional activities to get there. What counts as a task in the era of next-generation standards is, Goldman and Lee (2014) note, developmentally appropriate applications of the literacy practices content-area professionals engage in—thinking and reasoning, in other words, well beyond what is assessed on multiple-choice tests, worksheets, and so on.

In short, an instructional task includes both the work students are asked to do and the design that supports its completion. The scope is, as you might have noticed, larger than what you may be used to; rather than referring to an individual activity or assignment students complete within a single period, here a task includes all of the components of teaching and learning that take place over what is likely to be multiple activities and multiple days of instruction. The reason for taking on a more expansive, intensive notion of a task is so that the work students are asked to accomplish is worthy of this amount of instructional time. If students are to engage in the kinds of work associated with higher-order thinking, and not just pay lip service to the idea, teachers must design instruction that requires this kind of thinking. Students must learn to reason, develop precise language, and create arguments (Lampert et al., 2013; Sfard, 1998). Next-generation standards and assessments involve thinking and reasoning processes beyond the purview of traditional definitions of comprehension, so teaching these practices will be among the most difficult aspects of teaching. It only makes sense for teachers and students alike to focus more time and greater energy on this essential work.

Rigorous Learning Through Rigorous Task Design

Think of a high-quality task as being an act of synthesis, a fusion of standards, a discipline-specific inquiry, and a literacy engagement into meaningful learning opportunities. Start by clustering your standards. Which benchmarks, when combined with others, support students in engaging with rigorous content in the following ways (NGA & CCSSO, 2010)?

- Engaging texts and research to answer a question (including a self-generated question) or solve a problem (CCRA.R.7, CCRA.W.7, CCRA.SL.2)

- Synthesizing multiple sources on the subject to demonstrate understanding (CCRA.R.7, CCRA.R.9, CCRA.W.7, CCRA.W.8, CCRA.SL.2)

- Evaluating the evidence and reasoning of texts or sources (CCRA.R.8, CCRA.W.8, CCRA.SL.3)

- Drawing on and integrating evidence from texts to support analysis, reflection, and research (all, but especially CCRA.W.9)

If these qualities represent the core features or performances of a high-quality task, it follows that equally high-quality instructional supports are needed, most especially:

- Multiple high-quality texts

- Instruction on how to read, write, speak, think, and so on in ways that support completing the task

- o Activities that scaffold student understanding and proficiency
- o Assessments that demand students enact the work in meaningful formats and contexts

Teachers adjust the focus, length, and intensity of these supports based on student need and readiness.

Figure 6.1 provides an overview of the design process for high-quality instructional tasks that is aligned to next-generation standards and assessments and centers instructional work on synthesis. Notice how the design of a standards-aligned instructional task incorporates many standards, and that these standards are pulled not only from the Reading standards but from the Language, Speaking and Listening, and Writing standards as well; they are there not to cover more ground or create more work but as a way to facilitate student learning and enhance students' literacy experiences. Note, too, the accompanying teacher moves. Teaching of skills and content occurs *within* the process of completing the task—not as separate functions but as a means to support student work.

Each step of the design process links to the Common Core and is described in the following sections. If you are using a different standards framework, be sure and locate an equivalent or similar standard in your own set.

Step 1: Building a Foundation for Rigor

Common Core standards to address: CCRA.R.7, CCRA.R.9, CCRA.SL.2, and/or CCRA.W.7 and CCRA.R.10

To build the foundation necessary to support rigor, you must define the shape and rigor of the task by focusing on the standards that demand students engage multiple texts to solve a problem or generate claims (in the Common Core, this is the province of the Integration of Knowledge and Ideas domain in the Reading anchor standards) or that emphasize the review, evaluation, and integration of evidence (such as the Writing anchor standards in the Research to Build Knowledge domain) as a means to build and support problem-based learning. This ensures, from the outset, that students' work is grounded in problems of your content area and prompts higher-order thinking skills.

The two planning processes in this step, defining the intellectual or interpretive problem and developing a text set, are done concurrently; each helps define the other.

	Step 1: Building a Foundation for Rigor	Step 2: Supporting Student Engagement of Complex Texts	Step 3: Assessing Higher-Order Thinking	Step 4: Designing Activities for Higher-Order Thinking
Standards addressed	CCRA.R.10 plus CCRA.R.7, CCRA.R.9, CCRA.SL.2, and/or CCRA.W.7	Select one to two from CCRA.R.2–6, CCRA.R.8, CCRA.W.7–8, SL.3, and/or CCRA.L.3–5	CCRA.W.1 or CCRA.W.2 or CCRA.SL.4–6 plus W.9, W.10 plus Select one to two from CCRA.W.1, CCRA.W.2, CCRA.W.8., or CCRA.L.1–3, 6	CCRA.S.L1 plus CCRA.R.1 plus previously selected standards from step two
	$\longrightarrow$			
Accompanying teacher actions	• Define the intellectual and interpretive problem. • Develop the text set.	• Identify student needs. • Develop questions. • Adapt or excerpt texts.	• Design an analytical response. • Support the analytical response.	• Use strategy instruction • Develop inquiry frames • Use collaboration for learning

Source for standards: NGA & CCSSO, 2010.

Figure 6.1: A framework for Common Core–based instructional design.

Define the Intellectual or Interpretive Problem

Common Core standards to address: CCRA.R.7, CCRA.R.9, CCRA.SL.2, and/or CCRA.W.7

Experts who engage in inquiry—professionals, academics—begin with a question or problem worthy of investigation that turns into a goal, project, or pursuit; there's no reason why students shouldn't do the same. After all, the goal of more rigorous standards is not simply to provide students access to harder texts; it's to make high school students independent and proficient readers of college- and career-ready *content*—the kind that addresses, argues over, and aspires to solve the technical and intellectual problems your students will face as 21st century citizens. Centering the study of texts in your class on addressing complex, meaningful problems of your discipline positions your students as problem solvers and idea generators, builds student background knowledge, and better enables students to engage in the analysis, evaluation, and synthesis nearly all high school Reading standards demand.

The term *intellectual problem* is used here to create explicit lines of inquiry, similar to those that historians, scientists, writers, and critics use to engage their discipline and distinguish it from a guiding or essential question for a unit or year, which is the sort of overarching question that requires a minimum of several weeks or even months of ongoing study to address. Intellectual problems are more short-term. They arise from and guide interaction with specific text or content; they are meant to frame a single or several days of instruction. As rich and rigorous content, the complex texts you use articulate the key issues, questions, and interests of your discipline that you can address; your intellectual problems will arise from the content in them and the discussion about them. Following are several sample intellectual problems:

- How revolutionary was the Revolutionary War, really?

- What is the purpose of the unreliable narrator, and what meaning or value does it add to artistic works?

- What does Neil deGrasse Tyson's (1996) "In Defense of the Big Bang" suggest about proof and how we know what we know when it comes to scientific concepts?

These intellectual problems get at the heart of each discipline's ways of knowing: how to assess the significance of events or figures (social studies), how to analyze how writers convey aesthetic experience (English), and how to make sense of and evaluate processes (science). You can see how the examples run the gamut of possible approaches: from studying specific theories or claims (the first example) to making sense of general discipline concepts (the second) to developing or verifying one's own framework for understanding how experts think (third). You can also see how the questions dovetail nicely into the task. A science teacher might ask her students to trace how the author of "In Defense of the Big Bang" (Tyson, 1996) builds his case, and how that case compares to other theories in terms of strength of evidence and perception. A social studies teacher may address the "revolutionary" question by having students approach the text (see chapter 5) from various personas or theoretical lenses and then compare the possible assessments. The intellectual problem, then, is a way for teachers to leverage the text to support higher-level thinking.

There will also be situations in all content areas where the critical challenge is comprehending *how* language contributes to the content. Such an *interpretive problem* essentially problematizes literal readings of the text; it makes understanding the author's choices in expression and organization a kind of inquiry, one in which students study texts carefully and posit interpretations of form, intent, and meaning

(Lee, 2007). In essence, solving interpretive problems means conducting literary readings of texts (even when reading nonfiction). This includes recognizing patterns, making connections within and across texts, and inferring meaning when it is not immediately clear. Consider the following interpretive problems.

- How do President George W. Bush and President Barack Obama's conceptions of democracy and liberty compare? (RH.11–12.4, RH.11–12.9)

- How does the notion of a house function as a symbol in the works of Sandra Cisneros? (L.9–10.4)

- How do the structure and point of view of Neil deGrasse Tyson's (1996) "In Defense of the Big Bang" contribute to the persuasiveness of the ideas? (RST.11–12.5)

Note the inclusion of standards in the examples of interpretive problems. Solving interpretive problems should attend directly to the Craft and Structure domain in the Reading standards (CCRA.R.4–6) or Language anchor standard four (CCRA.L.4), which covers figurative language. The language and organization of the text, in other words, is the problem to be examined.

It should be noted that intellectual and interpretive problems are themselves no panacea for reading challenging texts. They provide students with a focus for their reading and analysis but do not show them *how* to read. A high-quality problem, in other words, depends on high-quality instruction and instructional activity to marshal the skills and methods to solve it.

Develop the Text Set

Common Core standard to address: CCRA.R.10

As discussed in chapter 4, text sets are clusters of multiple texts on the same problem, topic, or in the same genre that support cross-text inquiry and synthesis. Such sets are necessary to meeting the demands of the CCSS not simply because of the volume and range of demands of text-complexity expectations but because the standards, such as those in the Integration of Knowledge and Ideas domain in the Reading strand (CCRA.R.7–9), require students to compare and synthesize across texts in order to solve content-area problems (per the previous section). Selecting and applying texts is more than simply a matter of content; the text set must be a teaching tool, one that enables students to engage in increasingly more sophisticated content over time. That means choosing text types and specific selections requires careful consideration of not only the complexity of potential texts but also of the problems intended to be solved, the skills to be addressed, and student readiness—in other words, how the texts might contribute to student understanding. (See chapter 4 for an in-depth discussion of how to build a text set.)

Step 2: Supporting Student Engagement of Complex Texts

Common Core standards to address: One or two of CCRA.R.2–6, CCRA.R.8, CCRA.W.7–8, CCRA.SL.3, and/or CCRA.L.3–5

The Reading standards of your respective framework will have specific benchmarks that indicate what students are expected to analyze and evaluate texts for—such as central ideas, structure, figurative language, and so on—and are thus the skills you teach to support completion of the intellectual or interpretive problem. (In the Common Core, these are Reading anchor standards two through six as well as eight, Writing anchor standards seven through nine, and Language anchor standards three through five [NGA & CCSSO, 2010].) Prioritize one or two of these analysis standards (or components within the standards); you can address other standards indirectly through questioning and activity, but these are the ones you'll need to provide direct support for in order to help students understand the text. Which ones to focus on is determined by the demands of the texts, the components most likely to help students develop deep understanding and solve problems, and the most likely places or sources of student challenge with the content.

Identify Student Needs

Connecting the text or texts to be taught with the readers who will engage in the material is necessary to help formulate both instructional tasks and how to help students address them. As discussed in chapter 5, the texts must be read with an eye toward your students' experiences, projecting likely opportunities and challenges prior to and during classroom activity. This includes:

- Identifying challenging passages and vocabulary with which students should engage but will need support in doing so

- Considering what students do and do not know about the content or structure of the texts

- Analyzing texts in terms of where and how concepts in the standards selected are conveyed

- Identifying where and how the texts support addressing the intellectual problem

- Considering how the texts relate to students' prior knowledge and interests or previously studied material in your class

Aligning text with your readers and your curriculum ensures you can attend specifically and effectively to what the text and intellectual problem demand of students.

Develop Questions

To ensure students can address the intellectual or interpretive problem, supporting questions that scaffold students to higher-order thinking within and across texts are necessary. Developing these questions first, rather than the activity or discussion in which they might be used, ensures that they strategically lead students toward answering the richest and most complex intellectual or interpretive problems.

To develop questions that support student engagement with complex texts, start by directly addressing the demands of standards you have selected.

- Use questions that prompt evaluation or synthesis within and across texts. (In the Common Core, these are Reading anchor standards seven through nine and Writing anchor standards seven and eight.)

- Use questions that prompt analysis of selected components of the text language or structure. (In the Common Core, these are Reading anchor standards two through six, as well as eight, and Language anchor standards four through six.)

- Use questions that prompt literal comprehension about the text (Reading anchor standard one).

Note how these questions are in seemingly reverse order: you start by identifying the most cognitively challenging questions and then work backward by considering what would need to be known—and asked—to answer this question. For instance, to evaluate the arguments (RH.9–10.8) of the Federalists and Anti-Federalists in regard to the power and role of the central government, students would need to be able to distinguish the claims, evidence, and reasoning of each side, as well as construct criteria for what defines good governance in order to evaluate or assess the contrasting perspectives. Identifying these needs help us develop a frame or outline to construct the task.

Adapt or Excerpt Texts

Once it is clear what purpose the texts serve—for example, to assist students in addressing the intellectual problem—and once it is clear how students are likely to respond to the texts and what students will need to understand them, it will also be clear how the text should be used, and whether it will need to be modified in any way for students, as discussed in chapter 4. This may result in determining what parts of a longer text are most relevant to addressing the intellectual problem, or it may be that portions of the text are to be specifically focused on or avoided because of their complexity. It may also be that reading the text as a whole is most useful to students or that the use of a snippet of text, in conjunction with snippets from several other sources, best supports the kind of intellectual problem in which students are to engage. The point is to make decisions about what aspects of the texts students will engage in, and for what purpose, as a way to determine how students will interact with the text and one another to support development of deep understanding and application of that understanding.

Step 3: Assessing Higher-Order Thinking

Common Core standards to address: CCRA.W.1, 2 or CCRA.SL.4–6 and CCRA.W.4 and CCRA.W.9, CCRA.W.10

Typical curriculum development models advocate a *backward design* approach in which the summative assessment is the first product developed. The remainder of an instructional unit is backmapped from the assessment (Wiggins & McTighe, 2005). Given the popularity and commonality of this approach, why is work on the culminating product of the task located in step three here? It's simple: you have already created the assessment. In identifying the intellectual or interpretive problem, and in setting a general expectation for all intellectual work with tasks, the content focus of the task and the format have already been determined. Students will respond directly to or expand on the intellectual problem by reading multiple sources, synthesizing new understandings from them, and integrating evidence from the texts into analytical responses, and so on. At this point, what needs to be determined are the specifics of how students will demonstrate independent proficiency with the text and the intellectual problem—whether through writing or speaking (CCRA.SL.4) or some other performance, whether the product will be argumentative (CCRA.W.1) or expository (CCRA.W.2), what the assignment context will be in terms of the form, audience, and so on (CCRA.W.4). They draw on evidence from the texts they read (CCRA.W.9) to support their responses.

Design an Analytical Response

Common Core standards to address: CCRA.W.1, CCRA.W.2, CCRA.W.4, CCRA.SL.4

According to guidance from the PARCC assessment, secondary students should have multiple opportunities within a given unit or quarter to respond in writing to texts; these responses should reflect the formality of an essay or project assignment but be shorter in length and intensity—say, a homework assignment or a graded in-class assignment that students have twenty to thirty minutes to compose. The purpose of these multiparagraph—but not necessarily multidraft—responses is twofold: (1) for students to demonstrate understanding of the texts and (2) for students to demonstrate an ability to competently communicate in multiple forms in response to complex college- or career-level questions or challenges (the intellectual or interpretive problem). Such writing tasks are referred to as *analytical* because they focus on argumentation (CCRA.W.1) or explanation (CCRA.W.2)—not to mention CCRA.R.7–9 and parts of CCRA.W.7–9—and emphasize using evidence and logical reasoning to support positions or descriptions. Research is critical to academic success (Correnti, Matsumura, Hamilton, & Wang, 2013; National Commission on Writing in America's Schools and Colleges, 2003).

Analytical writing tasks include:

○ Responding directly to the intellectual or interpretive problem; for example, "Explain, using evidence from two texts, the purpose and impact of an unreliable narrator in fiction."

○ Composing parts for or a part of the summative performance assessment; for example, "Compose the conclusion for a formal essay assignment, or identify key pieces of evidence and why they were selected."

○ Comparing the features or meanings of multiple texts; for example, "Compare and contrast the use of unreliable narration in *The Great Gatsby* and *Rashomon.*"

○ Conducting short research investigations and synthesizing findings; for example, "Find two critical perspectives on the unreliable narrator, and explain how their insights enhance your understanding of *The Great Gatsby.*"

These features can appear in separate kinds of tasks, or they can be used within a single task. For example, students can do additional research to respond to the intellectual problem, or they can answer the intellectual problem considering how two or more texts address it. Note, too, they can address the tasks through speech or performance, thereby addressing Speaking and Listening standards (CCRA.SL.4–6 in the Common Core).

Support the Analytical Response

Common Core standards to address: Substandards of CCRA.W.1, CCRA.W.2, CCRA.W.8, CCRA.W.9, CCRA.L.1–3, CCRA.L.6

Culminating task work with an analytical response assignment enables all content-area teachers to teach *how* to write and speak analytically, a capacity that does not come easily to most high school students. Using the standards and an ongoing assessment of student needs and readiness, teachers can home in on the one or two appropriate writing skills that are necessary for students to know and be able to do in order to complete the assignment fully and effectively. Teachers teach these skills and coach and give feedback on their use before or during the response to the assignment.

Table 6.1 provides a list, per the Common Core, of these skills for both high school grade bands, grades 9–10 and grades 11–12; the skills are organized by the component of formal writing they address: claim or idea development, integrating evidence, organization, and style and correctness.

Table 6.1: Writing and Response Skills Taught Within the Task Completion Process

	Grades 9–10	Grades 11–12
Claim or idea development	• Introduce precise claim(s), and distinguish the claim(s) from alternate or opposing claims. (W.9–10.1.A) • Develop claim(s) and counterclaims fairly, supplying evidence for each while pointing out the strengths and limitations of both in a manner that anticipates the audience's knowledge level and concerns. (W.9–10.1.B)	• Introduce precise, knowledgeable claim(s), establish the significance of the claim(s), and distinguish the claim(s) from alternate or opposing claim(s). (W.11–12.1.A) • Develop claim(s) and counterclaims fairly and thoroughly, supplying the most relevant evidence for each while pointing out the strengths and limitations of both in a manner that anticipates the audience's knowledge level, concerns, values, and possible biases. (W.11–12.1.B)
Integrating evidence	• Develop the topic with well-chosen, relevant, and sufficient facts, extended definitions, concrete details, quotations, or other information and examples appropriate to the audience's knowledge of the topic. (W.9–10.2.B) • Integrate information into the text selectively to maintain the flow of ideas, avoiding plagiarism and overreliance on any one source and following a standard format for citation. (W.9–10.8) • Draw evidence from informational texts to support analysis, reflection, and research. (W.9–10.9)	• Develop the topic thoroughly by selecting the most significant and relevant facts, extended definitions, concrete details, quotations, or other information and examples appropriate to the audience's knowledge of the topic. (W.11–12.2.B) • Integrate information into the text selectively to maintain the flow of ideas, avoiding plagiarism and overreliance on any one source and following a standard format for citation. (W.11–12.8) • Draw evidence from informational texts to support analysis, reflection, and research. (W.11–12.9)

Organization	• Create an organization that establishes clear relationships among claim(s), counterclaims, reasons, and evidence. (W.9–10.1.A) • Introduce a topic; organize complex ideas, concepts, and information to make important connections and distinctions; include formatting (e.g., headings), graphics (e.g., figures, tables), and multimedia when useful to aiding comprehension. (W.9–10.2.A) • Provide a concluding statement or section that follows from and supports the argument presented. (W.9–10.1.E) • Provide a concluding statement or section that follows from and supports the information or explanation presented (e.g., articulating implications or the significance of the topic). (W.9–10.2.F) • Use words, phrases, and clauses to link the major sections of the text, create cohesion, and clarify the relationships between claim(s) and reasons, between reasons and evidence, and between claim(s) and counterclaims. (W.9–10.1.C) • Use appropriate and varied transitions to link the major sections of the text, create cohesion, and clarify the relationships among complex ideas and concepts. (W.9–10.2.C)	• Create an organization that logically sequences claim(s), counterclaims, reasons, and evidence. (W.11–12.1.A) • Introduce a topic; organize complex ideas, concepts, and information so that each new element builds on that which precedes it to create a unified whole; include formatting (e.g., headings), graphics (e.g., figures and tables), and multimedia when useful to aiding comprehension. (W.11–12.2.A) • Provide a concluding statement or section that follows from and supports the argument presented. (W.11–12.1.E) • Provide a concluding statement or section that follows from and supports the information or explanation presented (e.g., articulating implications or the significance of the topic). (W.9–10.2.F) • Use words, phrases, and clauses as well as varied syntax to link the major sections of the text, create cohesion, and clarify the relationships between claim(s) and reasons, between reasons and evidence, and between claim(s) and counterclaims. (W.11–12.1.C) • Use appropriate and varied transitions and syntax to link the major sections of the text, create cohesion, and clarify the relationships among complex ideas and concepts. (W.11–12.2.C)

continued →

	Grades 9–10	Grades 11–12
Style and correctness	• Establish and maintain a formal style and objective tone while attending to the norms and conventions of the discipline in which they are writing. (W.9–10.1.D, W.9–10.2.E) • Use precise language and domain-specific vocabulary to manage the complexity of the topic. (W.9–10.2.D) • Use parallel structure. (L.9–10.1.A) • Use various types of phrases (noun, verb, adjectival, adverbial, participial, prepositional, absolute) and clauses (independent, dependent, noun, relative, adverbial) to convey specific meanings and add variety and interest to writing or presentations. (L.9–10.1.B) • Use a semicolon (and perhaps a conjunctive adverb) to link two or more closely related independent clauses. (L.9–10.2.A) • Use a colon to introduce a list or quotation. (L.9–10.2.B) • Write and edit work so that it conforms to the guidelines in a style manual . . . appropriate for the discipline and writing type. (L.9–10.3.A) • Acquire and use accurately general academic and domain-specific words and phrases, sufficient for reading, writing, speaking, and listening at the college and career readiness level. (L.9–10.6)	• Establish and maintain a formal style and objective tone while attending to the norms and conventions of the discipline in which they are writing. (W.11–12.1.D, W.11–12.2.E) • Use precise language, domain-specific vocabulary, and techniques such as metaphor, simile, and analogy to manage the complexity of the topic. (W.11–12.2.D) • Observe hyphenation conventions. (L.11–12.2.A) Vary syntax for effect, consulting references . . . for guidance as needed. (L.11–12.3.A) • Acquire and use accurately general academic and domain-specific words and phrases, sufficient for reading, writing, speaking, and listening at the college and career readiness level. (L.11–12.6)

Source for standards: NGA & CCSSO, 2010.

Decisions about which skills to teach are, again, dependent on the nature of the task and the assignment students are asked to complete, the expectations for response, and the current level of readiness or student need evident from previous work. Be sure to include in your grading criteria the specific skills you taught and had students practice.

Step 4: Designing Activities for Higher-Order Thinking

Common Core standards to address: CCRA.SL.1 and CCRA.R.1 and previously selected standards (from step two)

To help students practice the skills and knowledge needed to solve an intellectual problem, design activities that fuse the literacy foundation (your text-complexity standard; in the Common Core, CCRA.R.10) with the rigor level you established (your analysis and synthesis standards; in the Common Core, CCRA.R.7–9, CCRA .SL.3, or CCRA.W.7–8) and the specific analytical skills (in the Common Core, CCRA.R.2–6, 8; CCRA.W.7–8; CCRA.SL.2; or CCRA.L.3–5) to be taught. We'll explore this process through the use of inquiry frames, strategy instruction, and collaboration for learning.

Strategy Instruction

Once it is clear what content and skills students need to know and the process by which they'll know them, you must help students learn *how* to know them. Higher-order thinking in the way it is valued in academic and career settings does not come naturally, and a good intellectual problem or supporting activity alone cannot engender it; it has to be learned. The source of that learning is you: you are the expert reader and subject-matter expert, and therefore are the best model from which students can learn.

That means making explicit the ways in which you want students to think and act in relation to intellectual problems and complex texts, including how to think about particular text features articulated by your standards framework (such as point of view) and how to think about the process. It may also mean helping students think in particular ways about the specific content being taught. This is done not by telling or lecturing but through guided participation activities in which you engage in literate practice jointly with students, incorporating social interaction and practice as they are learning (Lee, 2001). Such modeling of expert practice may include thinking through a particularly difficult portion of the text aloud with the students, or it may include, as Carol Lee (2007) suggests, using a short "apprentice text" that students can readily grasp, such as a film or text type they are frequently exposed to in out-of-school settings. Doing so allows students to try out higher-order skills (such as evaluating an argument or comprehending uses of figurative language) before tackling more complex texts. Whatever its form, modeling involves showing students how to read and write complex texts, providing immediate and ongoing practice with texts, and processing learning through reflective and metacognitive talk during and after practice.

Even though modeling typically precedes collective or individual engagement in an instructional task, it's among the last steps in the instructional design process precisely because it requires a complete perspective on what students are to know and be able to do, what they will be asked to do to demonstrate that knowledge, and how they are likely to respond to the task. Once this is known, it should then be clear the kind and extent of support students will need in order to engage in the task. What kinds of challenges are students likely to face because of the text and the task, and what do they need to know how to do to mitigate those challenges? The answer determines what you should model and how that instruction will unfold.

The following five steps will help you develop strategy instruction to support reading and writing of complex texts.

1. Determine what students need to know and be able to do to complete the task that they may not yet know how to do or do well. Articulate the link between the skill, concept, or process and developing a proficient response to the task, doing so in a way that is accessible to high school students.

2. Engage in the skill or concept yourself with the task or texts. Identify the steps you took to enact the skill and any challenges you faced or that students are likely to face.

3. Construct a student-friendly process or protocol based on your own steps, and test it out on another portion of the text or another text entirely.

4. Identify the specific portion of text to be used as a model. Annotate or mark up the text to identify the salient features or ideas you will make clear to students.

5. Develop the sequence of activities inside of the modeling, such as how you will introduce the skill or concept, what students will do during the modeling, and so on. Determine how students will engage in initial practice with the skill or concept before completing the task.

Inquiry Frames

Common Core standards to address: CCRA.SL.1 and CCRA.R.1 and previously selected standards

Frame refers to a sequence of engagement with texts that you can implement within and across tasks; it is the work students do with texts. This is structured inquiry through reading, starting with students' problem-solving skills and leveraging them through student-to-student interactions (Grouws & Cebulla, 2000), and structuring the experience so that reading supports thinking, thinking supports speaking and collaboration, and speaking supports writing—in other words, building proficiency and independence with texts.

A frame is not simply an activity (such as a jigsaw) but rather a way of thinking through content problems. The teacher embeds activities within the frame to support certain kinds of thinking, not the other way around. For instance, reciprocal teaching, an approach to small-group reading instruction, includes within its sequence of reading and student-to-student engagement a set of roles and responsibilities—including predicting, clarifying, summarizing, and asking and answering questions—that lays out both how students comprehend the text and the way in which they engage one another (Palincsar & Brown, 1984). The teacher makes critical decisions to facilitate this approach through the text, groupings, and guidance and support on how students will engage in the roles and responsibilities. He or she can apply the frame to any reading; in fact, repeated use allows students to internalize effective approaches to handling challenging texts on their own.

Reciprocal teaching is not specific to a particular content area; there are, however, approaches that reflect the specific disciplinary frames experts use to discern complex texts in their subject matter. A few are discussed here.

English

Judith Langer (1994) speaks of discussion of literature as a potential place for exploration as readers assume a series of stances to grasp the significance of a text. Referring to student probing of literary texts as "envisionments," she suggests that students can formulate deep understanding of texts by first formulating broad (global) assertions and questions, and then articulating individual (personal) reflection and response to the text. These initial understandings can support movement toward analysis of how the text functions, and its comparative merits. You'll note that these stances echo the structure of the Reading standards themselves in the movement from addressing the key ideas and details of the text, to interpreting craft and structure, to synthesizing and evaluating ideas within and across texts in the integration of knowledge and ideas.

History

Peter Seixas (2008) notes that historians engage in their work in six key ways.

1. Establishing historical significance
2. Using primary document evidence

3. Identifying continuity and change

4. Analyzing cause and consequence

5. Taking historical perspectives

6. Understanding moral dimensions of history

Some or all of these kinds of thinking could compose the core activities used to complete a task, as could Robert Bain's (2005) critical frame of *support-extend-contest* when students are to take stances on historical issues, or Chauncey Monte-Sano's (2011) analytic frame of *evidence-perspective-interpretation* when considering the claims made in a primary source. Note again how each scaffolds the engagement from literal to abstract or interpretive; students are prompted to consider content multiple times and in multiple ways, each more cognitively complex, in order to construct their own claims and interpretations.

Science

Science has long had a formalized inquiry structure of its own in the scientific method; a like-minded inquiry cycle is the *5E model* (Bybee, 1997), in which the learner is moved from activating prior knowledge and positing initial claims (engage), to gathering data (explore), to describing and drawing conclusions about what was gathered (explain), to posing responses to the intellectual problem or applying data to other situations or problems (elaborate), to self-assessing his or her and others' findings (evaluate). The Common Core standards for science and technical subjects make clear such investigations of text occur both in conjunction with—see Reading for science and technical subjects standards three, eight, and nine for grades 9–10 and 11–12—and on their own from the *doing* of science (NGA & CCSSO, 2010). Predictions and hypotheses, collection of evidence, and drawing conclusions work just as well with words as they do in the laboratory.

The previous examples do not represent all possible inquiry frames; there are many, and you may already have your own that will work just fine with complex texts. The key, however, is their strategic use, matching the frame to the intellectual problem and standards being addressed. Homing in on claims, evidence, and reasoning makes more sense when evaluating texts (in the Common Core, CCRA.R.8, CCRA.W.8, CCRA.SL.3), developing proposals and reaching consensus seems ideal for solving problems (CCRA.R.7, CCRA.W.7), taking various personal and critical stances on literary texts' meanings is logical when the standards specify the breadth and range of text study (see CCRA.RL.9), and so on (NGA & CCSSO, 2010). Inquiry, in other words, is not merely an activity, much less the outgrowth of one; it is purposefully utilized to enhance how students respond to the text and task and is as complex and meaningful as the text and task themselves.

Collaboration for Learning

Thinking verbally with others to solve problems can transform how students communicate understanding to themselves, making collaboration a critical tool in supporting independent, proficient reading of and responses to complex texts (Sfard & Kieran, 2001). Chapter 8, page 111, addresses in detail how to design collaborative conversations that enhance comprehension and independence.

One critical takeaway of the framework and process described in this section is the multifaceted and multilayered conceptualization of instructional rigor. Rigor here is not in the text or task assignment alone but rather a characteristic of students' *behavior* with that text or task (Beers & Probst, 2013). This, again, is the result of very deliberate plans for what students are asked to do, the content they do it with, and the structures and supports you provide to aid student effort. This is more than simply a set of steps or sequence, but rather a way of thinking, a synthesis of text and content, standards, assessments, and instructional activities toward the goal of impactful teaching that enables students to do meaningful intellectual work. As figure 6.2 shows, begin by positioning the instruction around engaging intellectually rich texts and problems. Then, develop the framework through careful consideration of the skills, processes, and practices needed to fully engage students.

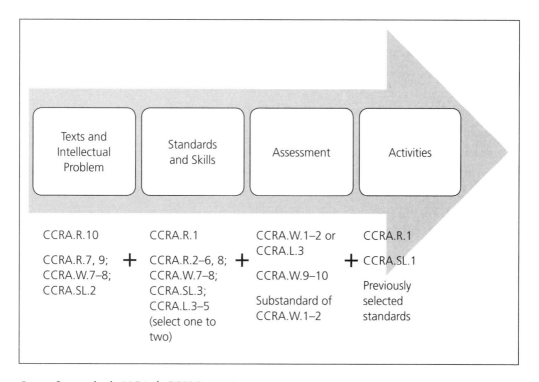

Source for standards: NGA & CCSSO, 2010.

Figure 6.2: Summary of the order of instructional planning.

A Better Unit of Measure

Focusing instructional time on the completion of high-quality tasks means some of the more traditional thinking about teaching may also need refocusing. First to go are individual daily lessons. A single, discrete lesson seems insufficient to support working with difficult texts, solving challenging problems, or developing independence. Rather, classrooms need structures that deemphasize incremental instruction and give primacy to significant practice, provide the time and the texts for students to engage in meaningful intellectual work, and allow teachers to scaffold this learning within and across tasks so the work increases in complexity and intensity. A module—the unit of instruction that includes the time, activity, support, and assessment used to complete a task—may be as short as a few lessons, if the class is closely analyzing a small section or component of text, or several weeks, if it is doing a full-length book study. On average, however, they are several days of instruction— enough time, essentially, to inquire into content-area problems, read part or whole of one or more complex texts, conduct short research (CCRA.W.7–8) or analytical writing (CCRA.W.1–2), and so on (NGA & CCSSO, 2010).

The term *module* implies both a self-contained segment and an interconnected part; modules form their own kind of mini-unit, with their own activities and assessments, but they are also connected with other modules to form longer sets of learning, helping students integrate understanding across texts and tasks. You can organize and bookend several modules with pre- and postassessments to form a unit or quarter of instruction. As figures 6.3 and 6.4 show, respectively, modules can be a series of ongoing steps and benchmarks leading up to a final performance, or they can each contribute a part to the ongoing completion of that end result. For example, if the goal is to have students compose an argument on a content-area problem, one approach, captured in figure 6.3, is to give them practice in smaller chunks (with each module) prior to assigning an essay or in-class writing prompt. Alternatively, as captured in figure 6.4, the modules might serve to address individual components of the culminating performance assessment, such as by helping students conduct research or develop a claim for the essay.

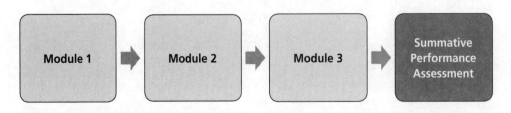

Figure 6.3: Sample unit where a series of modules builds up to a summative performance assessment.

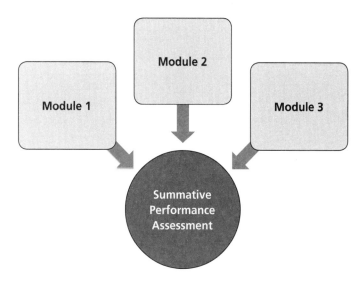

Figure 6.4: Sample unit where a series of modules contributes to a summative performance assessment.

These modules can be arranged so that what students are asked to read and do grows increasingly more rigorous, leading up to an extended and independent performance through writing or speaking of the performance assessment. The performance assessment itself can be a module with research minilessons and elements of the writing process (such as brainstorming, drafting, and presenting) spread over the course of several days of preparation, composition, and publication of the assessment task.

Think of modules as units within units, with standards and texts aligned across modules to support student growth in the core content and the skills being assessed. You can, in other words, keep the topical or thematic units that are already in your curriculum; the change comes in the deliberate sequencing and scaffolding of student work with texts and tasks high in rigor. Notice how in figure 6.5 (page 98), a unit on climate change is positioned to help grades 11–12 students learn in intellectually significant ways, from reading about science issues, to doing science, to taking stances on a science issue. Students experience a range of texts and tasks on the way to constructing their own texts in response.

This unit features both a pre- and postassessment to measure content knowledge and skill transfer. In between, it includes work around a small set of standards within each module and increasingly more challenging work with the same standards across the modules. A series of interrelated and authentic intellectual problems on the topic or issue guides the work, using a set of analytical writing tasks developed in class. The unit culminates in a formal writing assignment that serves as the summative performance assessment.

	Assessed Common Core Standards (including CCRA.R.1, 10*)	Texts	Intellectual Problem	Primary Instructional Analytical Writing Task
Formative preassessment	CCRA.W.1, CCRA.W.9, RST.11–12.2, RST.11–12.3, RST.11–12.8	"The Other Inconvenient Truth" plus mock directions for a lab experiment (Foley, 2010)	N/A (selected- and short constructed-response test)	
Module 1	RST.11–12.7, RST.11–12.2, W.11–12.7	"The Physical Science Behind Climate Change"; data from the National Oceanic and Atmospheric Administration; excerpts from "Climate Change 2013: The Physical Science Basis" (IPCC, 2013)	What are the measures for studying climate change, and what change has been measured? How do we know what causes change?	Summary of current data and understanding of climate science
Module 2	RST.11–12.3, RST.11–12.9, W.11–12.7	Laboratory instructions	How do we measure the composition of the atmosphere, and what do those measurements mean?	Laboratory exercise: measuring carbon dioxide plus a short lab report
Module 3	RST.11–12.2, RST.11–12.8, W.11–12.8	World Bank's *Turn Down the Heat* (World Bank, 2012); "A Grand Experiment to Rein in Climate Change" (Barringer, 2012); *Reframing the Problem of Climate Change* (Jaeger et al., 2012)	What are the near- and long-term consequences of climate change? What appears to be the most logical or likely most effective response?	Evaluation of solutions and recommendations
Summative performance assessment	CCRA.W.1, CCRA.W.8, RST.11–12.7, RST.11–12.9, CCRA.W.4–6	Unit texts plus outside research	What policy recommendations on climate change would you make to the next president?	A formal, researched essay or report

*These anchor standards are always addressed.
Source for standards: NGA & CCSSO, 2010.

Figure 6.5: Sample grades 11–12 unit on climate change.

In short, chunking instruction into multiday mini-units enables you to provide learning experiences in which students:

- Have multiple exposures to and practice opportunities with complex texts
- Respond to and solve authentic and meaningful problems of the given content area
- Receive guided support on how to analyze these texts
- Collaborate with peers on developing conceptual understanding of content from complex texts
- Demonstrate this emerging conceptual writing in speaking and writing
- Develop and support their ability to demonstrate proficiency on an ongoing or subsequent performance assessment

Next Steps: Planning for Instruction

Implementation of the framework for instructional design described in this chapter requires planning that reflects the instruction desired in classrooms. That kind of planning should be shared. As James Hiebert and Anne Morris (2012) make clear, structured collaboration on teaching is the most effective way to address shared instructional problems and to develop instructional products readily accessible for future teaching. The following steps will help get you started.

Analyze

Make an inventory with your peers of your current plans and resources. Ask yourself:

- What are we asking students to solve?
- How often?
- In what ways?
- With what texts?

This will help determine what you have and what you need.

Generate

Once it is clear what is needed, brainstorm possible solutions and additions to your existing curriculum:

- What intellectual problems of our content area can we address?

- What texts can support these problems?

- What kind of instructional support do we need to offer to support students solving these problems?

Plan, Enact, Revise

Begin to revise or construct individual modules. At the outset, go for the low-hanging fruit: adapt the novel unit, laboratory exercise, or existing instructional problem that already addresses some or all of the components in the instructional design process, and revise or add to ensure this work addresses the demands of the selected standards. Another logical starting place is to develop a module for the performance assessment itself, setting aside three to seven days of instructional time to have students closely examine or collect texts they'll use, to teach key writing or research skills for completing the task, and for responding to the task, such as by administering it as an on-demand in-class task or by using class time to peer review student work.

TEACHING CLOSE READING

Nowhere in the text of the CCSS is there explicit articulation of or reference to the term *close reading*; even appendix A, the addendum on text complexity, doesn't mention it (NGA & CCSSO, 2010, n.d.a). The closest the standards get to specifying or alluding to the idea is in Reading anchor standard one: "*Read closely* to determine what the text says explicitly and to make logical inferences from it; cite specific textual evidence when writing or speaking to support conclusions drawn from the text" (NGA & CCSSO, 2010, emphasis added). What appears to be a small distinction is, in fact, a critical implication for your work.

Let's start by being clear about what close reading is, since it's a term mentioned often in Common Core literature. *Close reading* has two common uses: (1) as a verb (to close read) to indicate a kind of practice and (2) as a noun (a close reading) to indicate a kind of pedagogy. In the former, as it has traditionally been used, *close reading* refers to a reader systematically reading and rereading a text in order to "investigate the specific strength of a literary work in as many details as possible . . . understanding how [the] text works, how it creates its effects on the most minute level" (Mikics, 2007, p. 61)—what Mortimer Adler and Charles Van Doren (1972) call "x-raying a book" (p. 75). In the latter usage, an idea spawned by the writers of the Common Core, a close reading is a kind of lesson in which the teacher spends significant instructional time—two or more days, often—walking students through a text, line by line or paragraph by paragraph, in order to unpack the literal and inferential meanings of the text (Coleman & Pimentel, 2012). Recommendations for conducting this kind of close analysis range from anywhere between once a month to three times a week.

Reading closely, however, might be thought of as process with purpose. Whereas close reading is engaging in a thorough reading of text to determine how meaning is deliberately conveyed through language, evidence, details, and organization, reading closely is engaging in a thorough reading of text in order to solve a problem or answer a question (see chapter 6). That is, students read closely in order to *do* something—to use the text to "support conclusions," as CCRA.R.1 says (NGA & CCSSO, 2010), in response to content concerns within and outside of the text. It is not, as a close reading has traditionally been made out to be, an instructional activity. It is an ongoing comprehension process led by the student and necessary to completing a task. This means it happens far more frequently than a close reading—in fact, it should be happening every day, multiple times a day.

Of course, a good close reading will include ongoing acts of reading closely; both intellectual and interpretive problems are solved through both close reading and reading closely. In both is the goal of enabling students to take a "critical-analytic stance," such that they can unpack a text's meanings, evaluate these meanings, and use the meanings to address their applications or implications for matters across and beyond the text (Wilkinson et al., 2010, p. 148).

But as a program for literacy instruction, much less as an instructional activity, adding or focusing on multiday close readings is neither comprehensive enough nor sufficient to ready students for college or career. This is because leveraging written text as a tool for thinking and communicating is a significantly unnatural act for most students (Wells, 1994); simply having students look closely at a text for a few days as something extra or tangential to core curriculum cannot be expected to change that. Expert readers read closely every day, and they don't do so because it's "close reading day"; their reading or sense-making doesn't follow some sort of template or question frame that can reduce the act to a ready-made lesson plan. No, reading is done with purpose and for a purpose, and filling instructional minutes is not one of them. You were not assigned to close read this book; you are reading it to be informed, to reflect on current beliefs and practices, and so on. Your engagement with this book is personalized, contextualized, and constructed; it is reading.

The point to take away from this distinction is this: reading closely is something to be learned and enacted daily; it is not a lesson plan but the foundation of your comprehension instruction. It is the work done to complete tasks, the process that forms the basis of student talk, and the access point for meeting standards. Such work, as the next section details, is achieved by paying close attention to the purpose, structure, and engagement of your design for reading instruction.

The Everyday Work of Reading Closely

Reading closely represents the ongoing work of students' engagement with texts—all of it. It is inclusive of a quick analysis of a word or phrase as well as a multiday close reading of instructional time unpacking a single paragraph or excerpt. Length of time doesn't matter—the kind of practice it enables does. This is a critical point because the new text complexity demands on what students read (and how much of it), coupled with an increase in expectation for what students do with texts (the cognitive rigor of the standards), increase the likelihood that students will need repeated exposure to the language and ideas of a text in order to grasp both its literal and inferential meanings. Reading closely, which is purpose driven, structured, and engaging, supports this very intentional work, whether it's five minutes or five days' worth of time.

Reading Closely Is Purpose Driven

CCSS Reading anchor standard one begins by noting that students will need to "read closely to determine . . . " (NGA & CCSSO, 2010). That *to determine* matters—it tells us that the reading serves to support student understanding and application of the text in certain ways, even when it just means grasping what it is literally being said. Purpose matters. Without it, students are doing close reading as an activity, not a practice. Teachers must clarify *what*, *why*, and *how* students are reading every day.

Guides on reading typically talk in general terms about the many purposes of reading—for pleasure, to gain knowledge, and so on—all of which are certainly valid. Here, however, the overarching purpose is rather single minded: purposeful reading instruction in high school prioritizes both understanding complex texts and synthesizing them into complex understandings of the world. It is what the Common Core means when it says students should "comprehend as well as critique" (NGA & CCSSO, 2010). Reading, in other words, supports engagement in meaningful intellectual and interpretive problems (see chapter 6), and the *why* of reading needs to be aligned closely with content-specific problem solving.

The following four foci ensure students are reading closely to engage in the text in ways that are up to standard.

Read Closely to Practice Specific Skills or Concepts in the Standards

Nearly all of the Common Core Reading standards require students to read text closely to understand what the text means and how it works. For example, consider RH.11–12.4, "[analyze] how an author uses and refines the meaning of a key term over the course of a text," or RST.9–10.6, "analyze the author's purpose in providing an explanation, describing a procedure, or discussing an experiment in a text" (NGA & CCSSO, 2010). It's only logical that you provide repeated opportunities to home in on specific features of the text whose complexity dovetails with next-generation standards. This practice serves to support students in understanding the individual texts they read, and it also provides them with the evidence they'll need to complete the culminating assessment for the module or unit.

Read Closely to Solve Interpretive Problems

As introduced in chapter 6, an interpretive problem is a kind of task that prompts students to attend to the meaning and usage of rhetorical and stylistic devices in a text (such as symbolism, satire, irony, and so on) that transcend literal or surface readings. For example, "How does a house function as a symbol in *The House on Mango Street*?" or "What role do parallelism and repetition play in enhancing the persuasiveness of Lincoln's Gettysburg Address?" Constructing such problems as a kind of inquiry, in which conversations about what the text means and how texts are open to interpretation, are critical to understanding the text's significance. They require students to read specific components of the text closely in order to articulate an analysis.

Read Closely to Synthesize Across Texts to Solve Intellectual Problems

Most close-reading exemplars focus exclusively on analyzing the language of the text, but students can also read closely to consider how an idea or argument is developed or compares *across* texts. They then can compare their conclusions to develop their own stance on a module or unit's intellectual problem. For example, students in a biology class might closely read two opposing views on genetic engineering, outlining the arguments of each and developing a qualified position that finds a middle ground between the two positions. Students in an English class might engage three short stories that deal with coming-of-age experiences, reading closely to identify patterns in how adolescence is captured in fiction.

Read Closely to Emulate Mentor Texts

Reading closely can also inform students' writing when teachers use *mentor texts*— that is, exemplars of ideas and form that students can emulate in their own work. In these instances, students read to understand how a text works—unpacking the specific ideas, the organization, and the rhetoric used by the author—and then practice them in their own writing. For example, students in a science course can look at an article in a scientific journal to see how sources are integrated into explanations or arguments. English students can study an argumentative essay to see how it is structured in order to write an argumentative essay of their own in the same style.

These strategies are not an exhaustive list of possible ways and means in which students read closely in the classroom; they are, however, ways in which reading addresses standards and supports completion of rigorous tasks. The intensity of the reading activity will vary. Sometimes, because the text has significant ideas or language, it will mean going paragraph by paragraph or even sentence by sentence; other times, because the work supports students' development of significant ideas or language, it will involve reading to ask and answer questions, to develop hypotheses or judgments, or even to just appreciate. Most times, it will involve a bit of all of these. Text and task determine how a student's ability to read closely is supported. The activity derives from the complexity, not the other way around.

Reading Closely Is Structured

Understanding complex texts on a deeper level requires careful attention to the ideas and language of the text. This is not natural for students, especially if the reason for studying the text is not immediately obvious. One critical scaffold, then, is how the teacher structures and sequences the reading experience in order to enable access to deeper meanings. Teachers can scaffold in this way by developing or utilizing a protocol for continuous engagement with content; each step is differentiated in terms of what students read, how they read it, and what they do with the text. Chapter 6 introduced this idea through the notion of *inquiry frames*—structured protocols for reading or problem solving that reflect what is used by professionals and experts in the given content area. Common close-reading processes, though not content specific, are a kind of generalized inquiry frame themselves, providing a structure for students to emulate the actions of expert readers.

Table 7.1 (page 106) summarizes the procedures of the four most widely known close-reading protocols: (1) the process used by the writers of the Common Core on their close-reading exemplars (see www.achievethecore.org); (2) the process described by Adler and Van Doren (1972) in *How to Read a Book*; (3) the process articulated by Richard Paul and Linda Elder (2006) in their book *Critical Thinking*; and (4) the process described by Douglas Fisher, Nancy Frey, and Diane Lapp's (2012) book *Text Complexity: Raising Rigor in Reading*. As you compare, consider the implications of these structures for your instructional support—what kind of structures do you need in your classroom for your content?

While listed in sequential order, none of the approaches in table 7.1 are intended to be conducted in lockstep; it is merely the general order the steps follow. In fact, facilitating the steps is often iterative, especially if you take them over the course of several days of instruction. Literal and inferential readings happen concurrently as the text progresses or in response to students' comprehension of it.

Table 7.1: Comparison of Four Popular Close-Reading Protocols

	Writers of the Common Core (Achieve the Core, n.d.)	Adler and Van Doren (1972)	Paul and Elder (2006)	Fisher, Frey, and Lapp (2012)
Step 1	Paraphrase or determine the literal meaning of the text.	Determine what the text is about, and classify its type and purpose.	Paraphrase the sentences or paragraphs of the reading.	Determine what the text says.
Step 2	Analyze the use of vocabulary, syntax, and figurative language.	Define the text's argument.	State the author's thesis.	Analyze how the text says it.
Step 3	Articulate how the text's meaning develops over time.	Critique the text's claims and reasoning.	Identify the author's purpose.	Articulate what the text means.
Step 4		Synthesize ideas across texts.	Assess the text.	
Step 5			Question the author.	

Sources: Adler & Van Doren, 1972; Fisher, Frey, & Lapp, 2012; Paul & Elder, 2006.

One significant takeaway from table 7.1 is that there is no singular approach to conducting an in-depth investigation of a text; the selection of one approach over another—or a different one altogether—depends on how the text is being read or the task in which students are engaging. For example, the Common Core and Fisher, Frey, and Lapp (2012) approaches seem particularly well suited to addressing interpretive problems and the Craft and Structure standards of the CCSS, as each focuses on analyzing how language within or organization of the text works to convey meaning. The Adler and Van Doren (1972) and Paul and Elder (2006) approaches, on the other hand, seem a more natural fit with connecting texts to solve intellectual problems and using the Integrating Knowledge and Idea domain of the Reading standards, as they prompt students to synthesize (CCRA.R.7, CCRA.R.9) or evaluate (CCRA.R.8), respectively, the text. Adapted or alternative steps are possible, too, including making text-to-self connections or having students take a critical stance on the text.

Table 7.1 does make clear, however, that these processes have some non-negotiables, chief among them rereading. You'll notice the focus is not on reading activities (such as a read-aloud or guided reading) but rather on what students will do with the text. The decisions about what and how to reread are yours. You can see that in all four models, the starting point is what I call the "gist read"—getting that literal understanding of what the text says and a surface-level grasp of its meaning. From there, students return to specific portions of the text—a word, an idea, a sentence, a paragraph, and so on—to consider how they contribute to the work as a whole. Finally, students consider the whole of the excerpt or text as a complete statement, articulating its meaning and judging its worth. Regardless of approach, any sustained reading work must enable students to engage in and demonstrate understanding of these three components: (1) the literal, (2) the rhetorical, and (3) the thematic or critical. Decisions about how to reread are deliberately planned to align with the demands of task and text and to increase students' existing understanding.

Reading Closely Is Engaging

The final point in planning effective engagement with texts is to focus student interaction during reading (and rereading) to ensure students are attending to and achieving the purpose. The key way to do that is through annotation.

As a dialogue with the text, effective annotation is both process and product; it is written sense making that emerges while reading, and it is the literal running record of a text (Probst, 1988). It helps students understand a text, allowing them to better answer text-dependent questions, and gives them an opportunity to practice writing. Annotation showcases students' abilities to cite, determine, analyze, and many other skills featured in the CCSS. Indeed, the idea that annotation is a form of assessment is being fully embraced by both the PARCC and SBAC, each of which include items on end-of-year assessments that prompt students to highlight on-screen features that support their analysis of a text.

Seeing annotation as both a process and product of understanding makes clear that merely underlining or placing symbols (such as a question mark) next to parts of the text that warrant interest or confusion are not sufficient mechanisms to enhance conceptual understanding of content, nor are they complete rigorous tasks. Rather, if annotation is to be a part of what it means to read closely, it needs to help students attend to the complexities of the specific text: the ideas and language that are the richest but most challenging to grasp. The way to do so is powerfully simple: task students with marking up the text for specific elements or purposes—the problem or question they are solving, the standards they are addressing, and so on. Instead of telling students to highlight or underline generally, a social studies teacher might ask students to specifically trace how the author of *The Warmth of Other Suns*, Isabel Wilkerson (2010), develops the idea that those who were participants in the Great Migration were not, in fact, migrants (RH.11–12.2). The teacher asks them to look specifically for evidence in the passage that connects with previous ideas or evidence (RH.11–12.1). They then cite this evidence (RH.11–12.1) in discussion or in the form of a summary (RH.11–12.2; NGA & CCSSO, 2010).

The point is to make annotation *the* act of comprehension. When finished reading a passage or full text, students review their annotations as a sort of rereading, using them to identify patterns and possible meanings and draw conclusions—a check and extension of their own comprehension (Porter-O'Donnell, 2004). Students then make their thinking visible by pairing with peers to share and check their findings, identify misperceptions or questions, and generate a new shared understanding. They also share the processes by which they come to these interpretations, articulating the strategies they are using and the text characteristics they are responding to (Goldman, 2012). Notice how this sequence is just that: a deliberate sequence to ensure and extend understanding. It starts with a focus on student understanding *during* reading. It then becomes a means for extending the initial reading and writing *after* reading through rereading, collaborating, monitoring, reflecting, and assessing through a writing task such as a summary.

In short, for annotation to be effective, it must serve as a way for students to articulate their emerging understanding. For annotation to be effective for teachers, it must focus on addressing specific learning objectives: product, not just process. Not only does such a focus eliminate highlighter syndrome (highlighting everything), but it also helps the student read with a purpose tied to critical aspects of the text.

So annotation should be a specific part of an instructional task—not a general process. That is, it should serve a specific role at a specific time during reading to help students analyze the ideas and language of the text. When reading a novel, for example, it doesn't make sense to simply ask students to circle or highlight aspects that sound important or are confusing. Instead, an English teacher might ask students to identify particularly evocative but ambiguous phrasings in the text, paraphrase them, and then explain how each contributes to their understanding of the text's characters.

Provide students with opportunities to review their annotations to check or extend their understanding. Following reading of the text, whether in class or as homework, have students review what they emphasized and wrote to verify they understand what you have tasked them to read. You can also ask them to synthesize their findings to respond to a new question or to generate a claim about what they have read. In addition, annotation improves collaboration. After independent reading, have students share and comment on each other's annotations, using the discussion to help clarify confusions about the text and reach consensus on the established task.

You can also incorporate annotations into formal writing assignments to support graded analytical writing work. In addition to having students better use text evidence

—after all, students have been analyzing the evidence via annotation—integrate the annotation work into the writing process by having students review their annotations to brainstorm and outline their response.

Finally, use annotations as a tool to guide instruction. By tying annotation to your learning objectives, you create data that can inform you right on the spot about what students know and can do. Monitor student work, including collecting annotation and noting where in the text students have difficulty, insightful ideas, and so on. Use their annotations to help determine future foci for reading.

Next Steps: Prioritizing Enactment

In fixating on close reading as a kind of lesson, the field of education seems to have given primacy to the technical components of improving instruction at the expense of the interactional ones. Such protocols may assist the work of teaching reading, but they are not substitutes for the complexity involved in enacting the work, especially not when inserted into a normal course of study as something extra. To emphasize *read closely* over and above *a close reading* means prioritizing enactment—that students learn content through their interaction with texts, and that this interaction must be continuous and continuously supported.

SETTING THE STANDARD FOR HIGH-QUALITY TALK

With the Common Core, collaborative discussion is more than just a good teaching practice—it *is* the standard, literally. Indeed, Speaking and Listening standard one for grades 9–10 and for grades 11–12 both demand that students "initiate and participate effectively in a range of collaborative discussions . . . with diverse partners on . . . topics, texts, and issues, building on others' ideas and expressing their own clearly and persuasively," making collaboration part of the comprehension process (NGA & CCSSO, 2010). This aligns with a growing body of research indicating that rich discussion can increase students' abilities to think about and learn from text (Beck & McKeown, 2006), students' engagement in reading (Guthrie et al., 2004), and the sophistication of their thinking, not only mentally or verbally but in writing too (Resnick, O'Connor, & Michaels, 2007; Sfard & Kieran, 2001). Interaction, then, can be thought of as a mechanism for learning; it is not just an activity, as we often think of when we plan for small-group work. It is an instructional support that, if designed strategically, helps scaffold students toward an understanding of complex material. Get students to carefully talk about texts, and it stands to reason that they'll be able to read, write, and talk about them better on their own as well.

Regardless of your feelings about the Common Core, Speaking and Listening standard one for grades 9–10 and grades 11–12 and their four substandards provide significantly more detail on the process of student learning—not just *what* students are supposed to know—than any other standard in the Common Core or comparative Speaking and Listening standards. This depth makes these standards an incredibly useful tool for designing student-driven inquiry of texts that supports meeting the expectations set by the Reading standards. As you review Speaking and Listening standard one for both high school grade levels in table 8.1, consider how the demands are also a means for enhancing all students' understanding and engagement. (Note: Skills and behaviors unique to each grade cluster are underlined.)

Table 8.1: Speaking and Listening Standard One for Grades 9–10 and 11–12

SL.9–10.1	SL.11–12.1
Initiate and participate effectively in a range of collaborative discussions (one-on-one, in groups, and teacher-led) with diverse partners on grades 9–10 topics, texts, and issues, building on others' ideas and expressing their own clearly and persuasively.	Initiate and participate effectively in a range of collaborative discussions (one-on-one, in groups, and teacher-led) with diverse partners on grades 11–12 topics, texts, and issues, building on others' ideas and expressing their own clearly and persuasively.
a. Come to discussions prepared, having read and researched material under study; explicitly draw on that preparation by referring to evidence from texts and other research on the topic or issue to stimulate a thoughtful, well-reasoned exchange of ideas.	a. Come to discussions prepared, having read and researched material under study; explicitly draw on that preparation by referring to evidence from texts and other research on the topic or issue to stimulate a thoughtful, well-reasoned exchange of ideas.
b. Work with peers to set rules for collegial discussions and <u>decision-making (e.g., informal consensus, taking votes on key issues, presentation of alternate views)</u>, clear goals and deadlines, and individual roles as needed.	b. Work with peers to promote <u>civil, democratic</u> discussions and <u>decision-making</u>, set clear goals and deadlines, and establish individual roles as needed.
c. Propel conversations by <u>posing and responding to questions</u> that relate the current discussion to <u>broader themes or larger ideas</u>; actively incorporate others into the discussion; and clarify, verify, or challenge ideas and conclusions.	c. Propel conversations by posing and responding to questions that <u>probe reasoning and evidence</u>; ensure a hearing for <u>a full range of positions</u> on a topic or issue; clarify, verify, or challenge ideas and conclusions; and promote <u>divergent and creative</u> perspectives.
d. Respond thoughtfully to diverse perspectives, <u>summarize points of agreement and disagreement</u>, and, when warranted, <u>qualify or justify their own views and understanding</u> and <u>make new connections in light of the evidence and reasoning presented</u>.	d. Respond thoughtfully to diverse perspectives; <u>synthesize comments, claims, and evidence made on all sides of an issue; resolve contradictions</u> when possible; and <u>determine what additional information or research is required</u> to deepen the investigation or complete the task.

Source for standards: NGA & CCSSO, 2010.

Based on the standards, it's clear that all students are expected to:

○ Be prepared to participate in a discussion

○ Set norms and guidelines for collaborating

○ Utilize evidence from the text to support conversation

○ Sustain a conversation by continually building on others' ideas

○ Reach conclusions and consensus, and extend individual and group understanding

This list, even as a broad summation, has meaningful implications for classroom instruction. "Come to discussions prepared," for example, indicates the need for students to have material to draw from in order to foster conversation, be it from a homework assignment or from an in-class quick write. The standard also shifts the ownership, at least within groups, for determining the structures and protocols for collaboration, asking students to determine how discussion should be structured, such as through goal setting and role-playing. It also asks students to be responsible not only for the outcome—whatever the task is they are to complete—but for ensuring a process that enables participation of all in support of that outcome, such as through questioning and building off one another's responses. Finally, students are expected to both produce an answer from the conversation and to go beyond it, whether by "mak[ing] new connections" (SL.9–10.1.D) or "determin[ing] what additional information or research is required" (SL.11–12.1.D) to address the task. Given these demands, it's clear that merely asking students to work together to complete a worksheet or answer a discussion question is insufficient not only to meet this standard but also to address the reading or writing standards in your standards framework.

The good news is that a teacher needn't look any further than the standard itself to determine what standards-aligned and standards-supporting group work should look like. The specific behaviors, identified in table 8.2 (page 114) as key discourse moves, make clear what to look for in student-to-student collaboration, and that, in turn, begins the conversation about how to facilitate this thinking and acting.

It's worth talking with your colleagues about these criteria, defining what they mean in your own words, and discussing the implications for instruction. To get started, let's tackle the most intriguing but ambiguous statement, the one that echoes all the way back to John Dewey (1935): engaging in "civil, democratic discussions and decision-making" (SL.11–12.1B). Dewey (1935) considered democracy as a kind of process—a "mode of social inquiry," he called it—that is realized through discussion and debate; it is deliberative. *Deliberative* suggests an ordered, civil way in which participants come to discuss and decide, one that allows for and even encourages

Table 8.2: Key Discourse Moves, by Grade, in Common Core Speaking and Listening Standard One

Key Discourse Moves for Grades 9–10	Key Discourse Moves for Grades 11–12
• Follow rules for collegial discussions and decision making (for example, informal consensus, taking votes on key issues, and presenting alternate views). • Pose and respond to questions. • Relate the current discussion to broader themes or larger ideas. • Clarify, verify, or challenge ideas and conclusions. • Summarize points of agreement and disagreement. • Qualify or justify views and understanding. • Make new connections in light of the evidence and reasoning presented.	• Engage in "civil, democratic discussions and decision-making." (SL.11–12.1B) • Pose and respond to questions that probe reasoning and evidence. • Hear a full range of positions on a topic or issue. • Clarify, verify, or challenge ideas and conclusions. • Promote divergent and creative perspectives. • Synthesize comments, claims, and evidence made on all sides of an issue. • Resolve contradictions when possible. • Determine what additional information or research is required to deepen the investigation or complete the task.

Source for standard: NGA & CCSSO, 2010.

disagreement as a way to focus the conversation with arguments and counterarguments, questioning, and consensus building. To have a democratic discussion, then, is to have one in which the procedural and the dialogic are heightened not only because participants would be "posing and responding to questions that probe reasoning and evidence" and "hearing . . . a full range of positions on a topic or issue," as other substandards of SL.9–10.1 and SL.11–12.1 indicate (SL.9–10.1.C, SL.11–12.1.C) but also because the participants themselves would be co-constructing the deliberation to make decisions, the decisions would be worth making, and the discussion would require a deliberative process to fully address the topic. Responsibility and participation would, therefore, be meaningfully and significantly shared between teacher and student and among students.

Overall, one of the stunning things about this list is how different its vision of student collaboration is from what has come to define typical *student-centered* activities in content-area classrooms. That is not to say that teachers don't do any or many of these things, but much of what passes for collaboration in high school classrooms is significantly product oriented: complete this, fill out that, jigsaw all of those. These criteria are not product oriented. Instead, they articulate comprehension as process and see that process as an instructional opportunity to teach students *how* to think.

How many of us can truly say we have regular routines (student-generated ones at that!) that enable sustained and intentional higher-level thinking among students? Group work would be more than an activity—it would be the most important and effective scaffolding tool a teacher could have: the student capable of and responsible for his or her own learning.

Developing a Framework for Effective Student-to-Student Collaboration

One obvious starting point on the way to improving the quality of talk in classrooms is to focus on what students are being asked to talk about. It shouldn't come as a surprise that the quality of talk is closely connected to the quality of problem solving and learning (Wilkinson, Soter, & Murphy, 2010). As the oft-quoted educational aphorism goes, "Task predicts performance"; the rigor and relevance of what students use talk for determines the length, intensity, and quality of how students engage one another (City, Elmore, Fiarman, & Teitel, 2009). If students are to do all of the things Common Core Speaking and Listening standard one asks for—developing protocols for conversation, sharing and sustaining conversation, reaching consensus, summarizing and synthesizing ideas, and so on—it follows that the tasks must not only be rich but also require collaboration that is not merely a way of engaging in activity but that actually enhances students' thinking and understanding. Simply asking students to talk more is no guarantee that they will *learn* more; what is needed is a particular kind of talk, the kind that is purposely designed to prompt student thinking and to make the verbalization of that thinking a kind of thinking itself.

That kind of talk is, in other words, *structured*; it is deliberately organized and sequenced, utilizing questioning or conversation protocols (such as reciprocal teaching and Socratic seminar) to develop student understanding (Resnick, Michaels, & O'Connor, 2010). It is also *instructive*. Such structured conversation, regardless of its form, requires certain kinds of discourse moves to ensure learning: higher-level thinking questions, extended elaborations, and use of questioning, both to and by students, that elicit inter- and extratextual connections (Applebee, Langer, Nystrand, & Gamoran, 2003; Taboada & Guthrie, 2006). Clark Chinn, Richard Anderson, and Martha Waggoner (2001) and the writers of the Common Core might also add *references to text* to that list.

Figure 8.1 (page 116), adapted from Andrew Wilkinson and colleagues' (2010) synthesis of the research on structured talk, provides a breakdown of the features of high-quality discussion-based instruction; it is organized by phases of student-to-student collaboration, including setting up for the collaboration, what occurs during it, and what follows it. As you review, consider how the findings correlate with the expectations articulated in Speaking and Listening standard one for high school or the corresponding standard in your framework.

Discussion Component	Research-Based Instructional Action
Setting Up for Discussion	
Choice of text	Teacher
Control of topic	Teacher
Facilitation	Teacher
Position	During reading, after reading
Grouping	Heterogeneous
Prediscussion activity	Yes
Participating in Discussion	
Format	Small group
Facilitation	Student
Interpretive authority	Student
Control of turns	Student
Assessing and Extending Discussion	
Postdiscussion activity	Yes

Source: Adapted from Wilkinson et al., 2010.

Figure 8.1: Sample framework for organizing discussions about texts.

The Setting Up for Discussion portion includes the curricular decisions the teacher makes in advance of the lesson and the frontloading planned in advance of the collaboration itself, including what is to be learned (texts, topic), when it is to be learned (position), and with whom it is to be learned (grouping). None of the findings should be all that surprising. The Participating in Discussion portion attends to responsibility and authority: who owns the conversation (facilitation, control of turns), and who generates answers and from where (interpretive authority)—students, in this case. Post-discussion activities can include (re)reading, homework, short writing assignments, and so on.

One takeaway from figure 8.1 is the correlation between the sequence of discussion-based instruction and ownership. The teacher is clearly the designer and supporter of instruction, but he or she is not the driver of it. That is, while the teacher makes a number of critical decisions about the purpose and content of the peer collaboration, the ownership of the ideas—what is generated and how they are generated—belongs firmly and totally to the students. Though it may appear self-evident to say that students should be responsible for what and how ideas are communicated in small-group work, in practice, teachers often underprepare students to engage in sustained and high-level conversation about complex texts and ideas and often overscaffold during small-group work. This framework suggests focus, emphasis, and support should be reversed. Instead, teachers should attend quite carefully to setting students up to *lead* these conversations—not only through inclusion of prediscussion activities like modeling or a writing prompt but by helping them learn to reason with one another through dialogue. Only then can students realize all of the components of Speaking and Learning standard one for high school, and only then can students realize full achievement of the Reading standards addressed during the discussion.

Getting Started With Discussion as Instruction

A quick glance at the components in figure 8.1 likely led you to make some immediate connections to your practice—perhaps to a discussion strategy (such as a jigsaw), or a particular activity you have used in your own classroom that meets most or all of the components listed. But you also know that utilizing a student-centered discussion approach and asking good questions are often not sufficient to sustain quality talk. For the kind of collaboration suggested by the Common Core, small-group work cannot be merely an activity; it needs to be part of *instruction*.

Teachers will need to provide ongoing support to initiate students into the kind of talk that promotes critical-reflective thinking; students, in other words, cannot be presumed to know how to "promote divergent and creative perspectives" (to give one example from SL.9–10.1) without teachers providing tasks that encourage and enable such thinking and showing students how to engage in such thinking. Teachers must teach students the routines of dialogue and provide opportunities to rehearse them every day in ways that demand the level of thinking and use of academic language necessary to succeed in postsecondary settings (Frey & Fisher, 2013; Sfard & Kieran, 2001).

The following guidance zeroes in on the means necessary to enact high-quality talk—the rules, if you will. While the research base identifies a litany of such teacher and student moves to support and enhance discussion (see Applebee et al., 2003;

Nystrand, 1997; Soter et al., 2008, for examples), the focus here moves beyond facilitation strategies to consider the kinds of planning and teaching needed to position students to engage in more extended elaborations, specifically through creating purposeful talk, structuring talk, teaching talk, and facilitating talk.

Creating Purposeful Talk

Often the use of small- and whole-group discussion feels self-evident: we use discussion because that's how it's always been done. But without articulating *why* you are using discussion, teachers risk facilitating instruction that does not address, or that even runs counter to, the learning goals of a given instructional plan.

Talk, then, shouldn't be used simply because it engages adolescents; it must be *designed* to move students toward independence on rigorous tasks. To start, make the link between activity and outcome explicit; discussion must support students answering the intellectual or interpretive problem. One way to do so, of course, is to make the problem the center of a small- or whole-group discussion. Discussion can, however, also set students up to address the problem on their own following the conversation, whether in the form of in-class writing or homework. Once you frame discussion as a means to answer or toward answering a rich problem, you can start to backward design instructional activities that lead to independence and proficiency.

Structuring Talk

With a clear purpose for discussion established, the next step is design: how can talk be structured so that students are released to independence? Answering this question means planning discussion intentionally so it can serve as a scaffold for student understanding. You must sequence instructional activities with increasing rigor and increasing movement toward answering the intellectual or interpretive problem. Students start by posing questions, clarifying ideas via course texts, and articulating what they know. They then move to testing or generating claims and answers, modifying and enhancing them based on discussion. Finally, to synthesize their understanding and that of others, they draw conclusions on the topic or problem. Table 8.3 shows how Common Core Speaking and Listening standard one for grades 9–10 and 11–12 can be organized as a set of steps or processes, each with increasing demands to reflect this.

SL.9–10.1 and SL.11–12.1 make clear that what students are asked to do during student talk and the intentional sequencing of these activities matters. A logical foundation to start from is a linear progression of cognitive complexity, as suggested by table 8.3: student talk activities can first focus on generating or responding to questions about the intellectual or interpretive problem, the text, and students' prior understanding. They also help students develop and expand a claim based on the

Table 8.3: Common Core Speaking and Listening Standard One, Organized by Task Type

	Grades 9–10	Grades 11–12
Clarifying and comprehending	• Pose and respond to questions. • Summarize points of agreement and disagreement.	• Pose and respond to questions that probe reasoning and evidence. • Resolve contradictions when possible.
Formulating claims and answers	• Clarify, verify, or challenge ideas and conclusions. • Qualify or justify one's own views and understanding.	• Ensure a hearing for a full range of positions on a topic or issue. • Clarify, verify, or challenge ideas and conclusions.
Connecting and expanding	• Relate the current discussion to broader themes or larger ideas. • Make new connections in light of the evidence and reasoning presented.	• Promote divergent and creative perspectives. • Determine what additional information or research is required to deepen the investigation or complete the task. • Synthesize comments, claims, and evidence made on all sides of an issue.

Source for standard: NGA & CCSSO, 2010.

questioning and evidence drawn from the initial engagement, and then support students in applying and extending their thinking to broaden their perspectives and make connections to the larger world. However, the order is not lockstep; discussion could start with students generating an initial claim (formulating claims and conclusions) or identifying needed research or data in order to do so (connecting and expanding). Student talk could, then, culminate in summarizing agreements and disagreements (clarifying and comprehending). The point is that students have opportunities inside of discussion activities to engage in all three phases of understanding, arguing, and synthesizing; the order will be dependent on the problem, the texts or content, you and your students, and your learning environment.

Once student talk is conceptualized this way, the relationship between the kinds of understanding needed to answer a given problem becomes evident. Such clarity also helps the teacher determine which discussion format to use and which activities support this understanding, as well as how these formats can be organized and sequenced to increase the cognitive complexity of tasks as instruction progresses. For example, to answer the intellectual problem of how revolutionary the Revolutionary War was (see chapter 5) requires students to know criteria for what makes an event revolutionary and specific aspects of the American Revolutionary War that might be used as evidence to assess it (clarifying and comprehending); to analyze and assess the arguments of scholars of history on the issue (formulating claims and answers, and connecting and expanding); and to formulate their own arguments, with evidence, in response to the problem (formulating claims and answers). Considering these cognitive steps toward solving the intellectual problem, a teacher can begin to think about the ways in which he or she can use discussion to support student independence. Perhaps a whole-class read-aloud of the anchor text is necessary to make sure students understand how the author defines *revolutionary*. Small groups might then analyze other scholars or primary sources to see if the definition applies. Finally, whole-class discussion could be leveraged to share assessments and identify a range of possible interpretations, leading to students writing a response to the problem.

Essentially, developing the kinds of discussions that lead to independence and proficiency require two kinds of structure: (1) deliberate sequencing of tasks so that students have corresponding supports as the cognitive demands placed on them increase, and (2) deliberate selection and design of discussion formats and activities to support student learning.

Teaching Talk

The discourse moves listed in table 8.2 (page 114) articulate ways in which students should attend to intellectual problems; tasks should ensure that students have these opportunities. But as descriptions of ways in which speaking and listening are up to standard, they also tell us that students need to learn how to enact these discourse moves—they are not natural, and activity alone will not ensure students master them. To "qualify or justify their own views" (SL.9–10.1.D), to "synthesize . . . all sides of an issue" (SL.11–12.1.D), and so on requires the same kind of teaching as it would if the skills were being taught for writing.

Since students typically are stronger orally than they are in writing, teaching discussion moves needn't be a long or particularly intensive process; you do, however, need to be *specific* by naming and modeling the discourse practice before setting students up to enact it. The activities should also be *interactive*, providing guided opportunities to participate in constructing and contributing to academic dialogue. A quick model or demonstration with students before initiating a small-group or whole-group discussion activity (such as a debate) can articulate the discussion expectations to students. Table 8.4 illustrates the steps and an example of such a process, using specific language from SL.9–10.1.

Table 8.4: Protocol for Modeling Discussion Moves

Steps	Sample Script
1. Name the move, using language from the standards.	An important way we use discussion to enhance our ability to solve the intellectual problem is by relating the ideas derived from discussion to broader themes or larger ideas. Doing so allows us to connect what we are learning on a single day to the work we are doing across the year and across your previous and future studies of the subject matter. To relate ideas to broader themes or larger ideas, we should ask ourselves and one another two types of questions. • The connection questions: What is the idea related to? What does it call to mind, and what does it agree or argue with? • The "so what" questions: Why is this idea important? What matters? Answering these questions together will help us uncover the key ideas underlying the texts we read.
2. Model the move.	Watch as I demonstrate with Javier. Javier, we've been talking in class about the common characteristics of dystopia in recent literature and film, but we haven't talked about why it is so popular in today's media. Why do you think it matters so much to people? Javier: "I think people like the idea of a world that's really different than their own." Teacher: "One thing that makes me wonder is if dystopia really is about our world, not merely the creation of a strange one. What does that make you think of?" Javier: "A lot of the dystopias we've talked about, like *The Hunger Games*, feature powerful and controlling governments. I feel like people are really distrustful of our government these days, and these books play off of it." Teacher: "Yeah, I think they really get at the anxieties we have in our world about losing our freedoms, or how technology might be used to punish or dehumanize us."
3. Discuss the move.	What did you notice about how Javier and I discussed larger themes and issues? *Students name what they saw and heard.*
4. Practice the move.	Now I want you to try it out. Turn to the person sitting next to you and continue talking about the significance of dystopias in our present world.
5. Provide feedback.	Nice work making connections to the works we've read in class. When breaking into small groups next, be sure and focus on answering the "so what" question to ensure your ideas get at the larger themes of our task today.

Source: Adapted from Wilson, 2012.

The protocol in table 8.4 takes no longer than three to five minutes to employ; students can then be released into pair-, small-group, or large- or whole-group discussion formats to apply the practice in pursuit of the intellectual problem.

A more inductive approach can also work. Have students engage in a discussion activity in which some students participate and others observe (such as fishbowl or Socratic seminar). Pause for a few minutes to ask the observing students to process and reflect on what they observed in relation to a particular aspect of Speaking and Listening standard one (say, "ensure a hearing for a full range of positions"), generating a list of behaviors or criteria that qualify as reflective of the specified skill. Then have students continue on in small groups to try out these practices, convening again following the activity to assess or revise them.

Facilitating Talk

Work on ensuring that high-quality talk does not end with planning; rather, the teacher's role and responsibility shifts to facilitation—to managing and maximizing learning inside of discussion. Here, we'll explore two facilitation approaches, exploratory talk and reasoning words, that pair well with next-generation standards for discussion and support sustained student engagement.

Exploratory Talk

More than simply exploring, the idea of exploratory talk connotes groups of students developing their ideas *through* conversation (Mercer, Wegerif, & Dawes, 1999). That is, discussion is directed or guided to be generative rather than merely confirmative or disputative. Students' opinions and understanding are not set; in fact, they may not even exist prior to engaging others in discussion. Conversation, then, serves as verbal thinking, which enables intrapersonal communication about what is being learned (Sfard & Kieran, 2001).

Because the reasoning develops *in* the talk, exploratory talk is marked by sharing reasoning. It seeks responses that are generative, marked by ideas that are not definitive or final. These statements are often longer and contain emerging, personal positioning, such as, "I think . . . " statements. Common features include:

- **Hypothesis generation**—Students collect and consider predictions and opinions ("What about . . . ") where ideas are not rejected.

- **Explanation of why**—Students share what led them to their initial predictions and assessments and what they are thinking as they listen to one another and generate their ideas ("What I'm trying to say is . . . ").

○ **Joint action**—Students make an initial shared decision, whether on the idea under discussion ("We all agree that . . . ") or on the next steps ("We need to find out why . . . ").

Exploratory talk hinges on creating an environment in which students feel comfortable thinking spontaneously *and* do so effectively. Because such talk acts as a springboard toward a more complete understanding, it's critical to give students a minute or two to develop a process for engaging one another, such as by indicating how students will share or by delegating roles to group members. This should occur before students read or reread the selected text to ensure they can flow right from reading into processing what they are reading. After student discussion roles are settled, the teacher introduces the tasks, which encourage initial interpretations and assessments, such as by taking a stance, declaring a position, or interpreting abstract language; these tasks should immediately follow rereading and be followed by further activity that allows students to confirm their initial thinking, look to the text for further evidence and clarification, and address more challenging questions or content.

Ideally, then, exploratory talk is brief and lively; take care not to make it routine. When first engaging in it, a quick fishbowl discussion with a group of students can illuminate the diversity and openness of sharing ideas, as well as the ways in which sharing can be reciprocative and nonconfrontational. Subsequently, it may help to give students a starting sentence stem, such as "My initial reaction is . . . " or "Here's what I'm thinking . . . " to help initiate the conversation. To extend or solidify initial reasoning, it might also help to have students verbalize their idea first, and then have them attempt to restate this idea in writing.

Reasoning Words

Reasoning words are the words and phrases that support the development of explanations, arguments, and conclusions. *Support* is the key here; these words—often conjunctions or modals (words, like *might*, that express the degree or force)—frame content in ways that allow others to respond, thereby extending the elaborations of group members.

Anna Soter and her colleagues (2008) found that three types of reasoning words are most prevalent in the critical-analytic approach to text discussion than any other:

1. Speculating or proposing words that frame hypotheses and interpretations

2. Positioning or claiming words that frame stances or levels of agreement

3. Analyzing or generalizing words that frame explanations

Table 8.5 (page 124) provides examples for each type of reasoning word. These reasoning words can also be used in question format.

Table 8.5: Examples of Reasoning Words

Reasoning Word Type	Examples
Speculating or proposing	*Would, could, maybe, if*
Positioning or claiming	*I agree, I disagree, I would argue*
Analyzing or generalizing	*Because, so, how, why*

Most students already use the words in table 8.5 quite frequently in conversation, and many of these words don't need explicit instruction, much less an introduction. Why, then, are they so critical for high school students to master? Because, as the language throughout the Common Core (and especially in CCRA.R.10) indicates, to be college ready means to independently make and analyze claims and proposals with complex texts—in other words, to reason mentally and in speaking and writing. Conversation with peers is a form of practice to scaffold more demanding and independent usage (such as a formal essay) later.

But simply asking students to use phrases like *because* or *I agree* more will not sufficiently enhance their ability to reason, much less sustain conversation for any significant length of time. Use of language is dependent on the quality and frequency of opportunities to practice: students can get better at internalizing and incorporating the language of analyzing and making claims if they're offered repeated practice at positioning, speculating, and analyzing. You could organize peer discussions accordingly: have students make initial predictions, claims, or evaluations; select evidence and provide support for their explanations; and then, finally, reach conclusions or consensus. Even better, teach students how to generate their own protocols and prompts that utilize the three question types from table 8.5, such as knowing to turn to a classmate and say, "Do you agree with that?" or "What do you mean by what you just said?"—so that the students, not the teacher, push others to explain their reasoning about the text.

Next Steps: Listening as a Kind of Teaching

The fact that Common Core Speaking and Listening standard one (both the anchor standard and the grade-level standards) shifts significant responsibility for facilitating and sustaining discussion to students does not, in fact, lessen the need for effective *teaching*; it does, however, shift the kind of teaching needed to support learning. That, as this chapter has discussed, includes better tasks, better modeling of how to talk, and better support during peer collaboration. However, helping students learn to talk more effectively also requires teachers to *listen* better.

The listening suggested here is qualitatively different from what the field of education has typically expected of teachers. In that vision, the teacher solicits and evaluates students' responses; listening is simply a byproduct of questioning. The kind of listening discussed here, however, gives primacy to cultivating student thinking and providing high-quality opportunities for students to think about and articulate their ideas at the forefront. Teaching through listening begins, then, with a deep fascination with students' ideas and a desire to build instruction around eliciting them. In practice, it means providing intellectually rich problems for students to solve and forums—small group and whole class—in which students can generate ideas and hone them verbally, with students continually describing not only what they know but also the thought processes behind their knowledge.

As mentioned previously, the most radical thing about this principle is how unradical it truly is: it puts students at the center. In fact, *they* become the curriculum. Careful attention to students' thinking can't help but guide our instructional decision making and inform our choice of problems, our questions to elicit their understanding, and our ways to help students solve and communicate the problems. The results of putting student thinking at the core of educators' work, as Elizabeth Fennema and her colleagues (1996) find, are quite impressive: when teachers' knowledge of their own students' thinking grows, their subject-matter knowledge and teaching efficacy grow in tandem. This doesn't require more professional development or knowing new instructional strategies; rather, it requires teachers to be open to and focus on what students can teach us about what they know. It's a shift, to be sure, but all of the answers are already in your classroom and the classrooms of your colleagues. Give yourself the opportunities during teaching to really concentrate on what students are saying—acknowledge it, build off of it, and encourage more of it. Teach to *listen*.

MOVING COLLABORATION TO THE CORE

Uncertainty around teaching with new standards is inevitable, as an evidence base for expert practice remains elusive. However, this gap creates the opportunity for teachers and schools to embrace exploration, practice, and reflection and to inquire about and design best practices rather than simply accumulate them. Implementing next-generation standards means not simply teaching but *learning*, too.

Thus, no vision for supporting the enactment of next-generation standards can require expertise to simply be imposed. We can't improve instruction merely by being informed about instructional improvement. We must improve instruction itself, and this work takes place *in* classrooms and *for* classroom practice. Research confirms that the most effective professional learning is focused on the work of teaching and is situated in the context of that work: teachers working together to study their actual teaching practice (the work of teaching) in and about the sites and settings in which they teach (their context; Borko, Jacobs, & Koellner, 2010; Desimone, 2011). With such a practice-centered vision, teachers regularly participate in intentional, structured mentoring and coaching; learn, observe, and rehearse teaching practices; analyze student work; and collaboratively develop new curriculum and assessment (Glazer & Hannafin, 2006; Grossman, Wineburg, & Woolworth, 2001; Hertzog, 2002). Beyond simply imparting *instrumental* knowledge—to know new things about teaching or new ways of teaching—professional development that focuses on practice advances the development of the mindset and problem-solving capacity critical to helping teachers respond to complex and uncertain teaching situations. In other words, it helps them implement the next-generation standards.

But why, when so many other things demand the precious minutes of staff-development time, should we focus collaboration specifically on literacy instruction? Many of the features associated with traditional high school literacy instruction—the privileging of textbooks, the overreliance on teacher-directed instruction, unchallenging projects, and so on—are the result of a lack of opportunity to not just learn about alternative approaches but also to enact them in meaningful ways. Focusing your professional learning time on literacy instruction counteracts this implementation gap by attending specifically to teachers' instructional practices: by investigating professional and content-area texts as both readers and educators, developing common curriculum to address these texts, practicing teaching literacy, studying readers to improve delivery of instruction, and so on (Clary, Styslinger, & Oglan, 2012; Lent, 2007). In this sense, a focus on literacy instruction is not something extra or in addition to existing collaboration—it *is* the collaboration.

Of course, the quality of such collaboration is directly related to the quality of the community in which it occurs. The collaboration must be aligned to ensure the work is being done in the right setting, the one closest to and most focused on daily instruction: your grade-level or course team. This forum best matches teacher readiness levels, is most conducive to knowledge sharing, and is most immediate to practice; it is the place in which next-generation standards implementation thrives or dies. Knowledge of teaching with the next-generation standards is not sufficient. It is the *way* of knowing that builds collective capacity. Expertise comes through high-quality interaction with content—in this case, you and your colleagues' own teaching—and purposeful practice of the essential components; knowing is an ongoing learning process, not just an outcome.

Such learning does not just happen; it is designed. To culminate this section's focus on classroom practice, I provide one possible vision for how teachers might work together to identify, study, plan, implement, and reflect on classroom implementation. Think of it as a foundation for your ongoing work that can be adapted depending on the experience, needs, and opportunities of your learning community.

Inquiry as Implementation: The Inquiry Cycle

I use the term *inquiry cycle* to consciously highlight the need for investigation and problem solving that drives both the purpose of the proposed learning structure and the actual learning taking place. There is very little fixed knowledge about the CCSS other than the language of the standards itself. There is little consensus yet on what best practice regarding these standards is. Exploring such unknowns empowers teachers and schools to develop instructional solutions that fit the particular needs of the students and communities they serve, including their own professional learning communities.

The visual-spatial order of the cycle described in figure 9.1 should look and feel familiar: it's a typical continuous flow diagram, with typical components—analysis, design, implementation, and evaluation—describing the process. What's atypical is that the process is led by teachers and centered on their interests and needs, it's rooted in standards, and it focuses learning about teaching through learning and teaching.

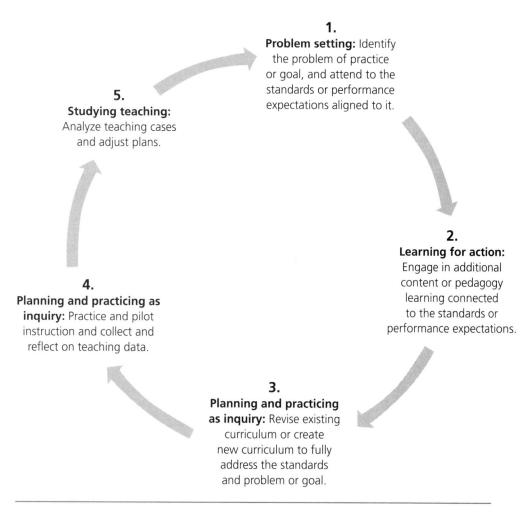

Figure 9.1: The inquiry cycle.

Each component of the process is detailed here, including how one high school team—in this case, a science content team—engages in inquiry throughout the process.

Step 1: Problem Setting

The cycle initiates with a goal or problem by looking at a particular standard or standards to articulate student outcomes; by identifying a particular problem of practice (such as sustaining student engagement during a close reading); or by reaching consensus on a desired instructional goal (such as developing a consensus approach to teaching annotation). Such a focus is based on the specific needs, interests, and readiness levels of the group. It may come from conversation and questioning from within the learning community, or it may be the result of an external source or mandate (such as a schoolwide initiative). Whatever the focus of the inquiry, the first step must begin with reviewing—even if you have seen it a hundred times before—the stated performance expectations for students (the Common Core or other next-generation standards) and teachers (the school's instructional framework) in the identified focus area; unwrapping ambiguous or confusing language in the performance expectations; assessing the current state of practice in the area; and then identifying next steps for increasing practitioner capacity.

To address a question like "How do we sustain student engagement during a close reading of a science text?" a group of physics educators might start by taking a closer look at standards such as Common Core Speaking and Listening standard one (SL.11–12.1.B)—since it addresses how students would engage one another in talking about texts—to unpack what it means for upperclassmen to sustain "civil" and "democratic" dialogues (NGA & CCSSO, 2010). You might consult elements 3b and 3c of the Framework for Teaching (Danielson, 2011)—or whatever instructional framework your school or district utilizes—to identify teaching practices deemed proficient to engage students. From there, our science teachers decide that further study of ways to increase student-led or student-to-student discourse is necessary to answer the initial guiding question.

Step 2: Learning for Action

Grounded in a shared purpose and pursuit, teams expand their understanding of the problem or question they identified by building a common language for understanding and acting on the standard, problem of practice, or instructional goal. The kind and intensity of this learning is dependent on the structures available to your collaborative group; it can be as specific and short as reviewing a single assessment item or discussing a brief professional reading, or it can be as broad and lengthy as observing instruction in other classrooms, or reviewing curriculum documents for adoption or deletion. (The reading to teach approach discussed in chapter 5 is an example of the latter.) The physics teachers, who are attempting to enhance student engagement with close reading, first read and discuss this book's chapter on productive talk (chapter 8) and then observe a colleague's instruction—either in the classroom or via video—to discuss opportunities and challenges for student-to-student interaction when studying texts.

While the methods will vary, the point remains the same: teachers dedicate time and focus to exploring a specific content or pedagogical area together to ensure learning is shared, not prescribed. It is this learning that enables teachers to then take a critical eye to existing instructional plans or to design new curriculum with a clear sense of the standard or performance goal in mind. You should expect and hope for both, given that expanding one's understanding of a concept should lead to both refinement of existing beliefs and practices, adoption of new ones, and dismissal of old ones.

Steps 3–4: Planning and Practicing as Inquiry

With your background knowledge increased and a common understanding among role-alike colleagues achieved, team attention can turn to practice—to implementing what has been learned. The favored method here is adapted from a professional development model—lesson study—in which a group of teachers prepare, present, and revise instructional plans together to determine best practice (Fernandez & Yoshida, 2004; Lewis, 2002). Beyond the opportunity to develop instruction with peers, practice this instruction, and reflect and revise, what is particularly effective about the method is how well it attends to the current readiness level of teachers. Since many teachers have simply not engaged in practices like text-based inquiry, the process can be used to develop supports for specific instructional needs or gaps in relation to the standards. Over time, groups of teachers can build a full compendium of tested and approved practices —a curriculum—aligned to next-generation standards.

Typically, to complete a lesson study—and the remainder of the steps in our inquiry cycle—teachers do the following.

1. Set goals for student learning and select texts.

2. Study supporting content (such as the relevant CCSS standards, existing curricula, texts to be taught, and so on).

3. Brainstorm how the lesson might be structured and reach consensus as a team on the lesson structure.

4. Practice the lesson and anticipate student misperceptions, and revise as needed.

5. Prepare the lesson for teaching (create handouts, format the lesson, and so on).

6. Implement and observe the lesson.

7. Debrief about the lesson.

8. Revise the lesson.

To begin, teachers develop objectives or learning targets for the lesson in the format typically used by teachers in your school (such as SWBAT [students will be able to] and the like). They next look at existing content and parameters related to the lesson goal—such as their previous attempts to teach the concept or skill—in order to develop or clarify expectations for what the lesson might look like. Once the focus is clear to all, teachers independently develop an initial lesson plan, including the specific problems or tasks they will use. Group members then come together and share their individual plans, using a review of all the plans to come to consensus on the single best way of how to teach the lesson—whether by voting for one teacher's plan, or by combining elements of multiple plans. Next they actually try out the lesson together—whether by doing a walkthrough or by attempting to solve the problems they created—in order to identify and to anticipate student difficulties. Then they revise the lesson and prepare for delivery, such as by devising handouts or creating a physical lesson plan document. The cycle moves into the next stage with the implementation of the lesson, which includes data collection (such as student work and observational data) by the teacher or observing teachers. The team then conducts a follow-up meeting to discuss what they learned, what should change, and how the group should move forward.

All of these actions are adjustable to the demands of the content and the individuals on the team. For example, a team might spend considerable time generating lesson goals and content. Alternatively, teachers may be given the goals and content by a school or district's instructional leaders and asked to work with specific objectives or content in mind. Teachers could work independently on their lesson at first so that they can examine several instructional approaches. Or perhaps everyone works on the same lesson from the outset. When delivering the lesson, a group can choose to all implement the lesson, or they can choose to have one teacher demonstrate and the others observe. The data collected may vary based on what teachers are trying to find out, though student performance data—even if they are just recorded evidence of students' verbal responses—almost always have a critical role in the discussion.

Our physics team, whose members want to support student engagement during a close reading of a text, select "The Mysteries of Mass" by Kane (2005) in *Scientific American*. A cursory read of the text suggests a key skill area—and, thus, a learning goal—is understanding how authors, which is also mentioned in the Common Core standard RST.11–12.6, "Analyze the author's purpose in providing an explanation, describing a procedure, or discussing an experiment in a text, identifying important issues that remain unresolved" (NGA & CCSSO, 2010). Since the text is a new addition to their coursework, further study of its content is necessary, and the team members engage in a close examination of the text in order to familiarize themselves with its ideas and make instructional decisions. Discussion about the text reveals the richest opportunity for discussion is in the "identifying important issues that remain unresolved" component of the standard, so they determine the best part of the text with which to address this and agree to each develop a lesson plan around that excerpt. When they reconvene, the team reviews the proposed lessons. Team members agree that teaching and practicing the "questioning the author" strategy would be most helpful to students and most likely to sustain student engagement (Beck et al., 1998). Only one teacher feels comfortable with teaching the approach, so the team decides to observe her teaching. Each team member will sit with a small group of students during the activity and take notes on what they see and hear. The exit slip the teacher uses to assess understanding will also be used in the team's debriefing of the lesson.

Step 5: Studying Teaching

Following the completion of initial teaching practice, teachers reconvene to review and respond to the teaching they enacted and observed, using data collected during the teaching—video, observations, and student work, primarily—to draw conclusions about their work. The participating teachers examine the teaching to make sense of what happened; assess what they know or can conclude about the larger issues at work (for example, any problems of practice or with the larger instructional goal); and propose future action. Using the data, they discuss:

- o **Task**—What were students asked to do, and how did the teacher present it to them or prepare the content for them?

- o **Engagement**—How did students respond to certain elements or activities in the task? What sense—or lack thereof—did they make of the content? How do we know?

- o **Understanding**—In what ways and to what extent does the end result or product of the students' work on the task demonstrate the established or expected outcomes?

As these questions suggest, the focus of the debriefing is on teaching and learning—what can we deduce from behaviors of teachers and students *during* instruction, and what does it mean for future implementation of the lesson or others like it? Answers to these questions help teacher teams determine how to revise or adapt the lesson, what new or additional problems of practice to focus on in future collaboration, and procedures to implement in their collaborative unit or their classrooms. The group then begins the cycle anew by either continuing the existing learning focus or moving on to another one.

Our physics team returns from watching one colleague's teaching to discuss what members learned and agree on some subsequent action steps. Because the questioning the author strategy was novel to some team members, they first consider what they observed about how the lesson tasks were set up and what they saw in small groups in response to the activities. They next look at what they observed about student understanding, considering both what students said in groups and what they produced on their exit tickets in relation to the text content and goals (the standard). As a result of these conversations, the group decides to modify the questioning-the-author strategy. It also agrees to assign students roles within small groups. The group discusses how structured talk that supports analysis and evaluation of text is the general solution to its question of "How do we sustain student engagement during a close reading of a science text?" but decides that it needs further study of these options before aligning them with common practice. Team members agree to select and study the teaching of another text during the next inquiry cycle in order to continue their learning.

The inquiry cycle process is precisely that: a process. Yes, it's complex and time intensive, taking a few days or sessions to complete, and it's not comprehensive—at least not at first. That, however, is a strength. Over time, teams will build a lexicon of collective best practice; in the meantime, teachers have continued opportunities to use and reflect on what they learned in the lesson study in their own individual teaching.

No staff-development system is perfect or limitless, and modifications will be necessary to align the process with your needs, including the frequency and length of your collaboration time, the focus of your work, the readiness of your team, and so on. Regardless of these decisions, the essential work is the same: study your teaching, even if such work can only happen once or twice a quarter.

The idea of professional development—but, really, *teaching*—as inquiry attacks the unfortunate irony limiting many existing teacher-development practices. Teachers are expected to become experts by accumulating experience, yet that same experience is often neglected or devalued. Models of professional learning that prioritize a knowledge base supposedly outside teachers' existing practice privilege the few at the expense of collective capacity and continuous improvement; the inquiry model presented here, on the other hand, seeks to be intentional about sustaining and enhancing reflective practice from the classroom outward, honoring and giving primacy to the practitioner.

In introducing text complexity, close reading, and other components of rigorous literacy instruction, the field of education seems to have given priority to the technical components of improving instruction at the expense of the relational ones—not only in terms of how to engage young readers but also in how colleagues engage one another in supporting their students. However much easier the technical components may be to facilitate, it is the latter—the relational components—that hold significantly greater potential to be transformative. Creating a vision for, and structures in support of, teachers as literacy learners and leaders rather than as receptacles for experts' knowledge or isolated chunks of practice puts students and teachers at the center of the work, making the richness of the process commensurate with the complexity of the intended product. Indeed, in the work teachers do to support literacy, and the literacy support schools offer teachers to do the work, practice must serve practice. Teachers will enact complex literacy practices if and only if they are engaging in and enacting complex texts and the associated practices together. Instructional planning only improves when it stems from and directly addresses the complexities of the text, not from an activity or content an individual teacher might be inclined to favor. Everything about teaching, then, would be subject to a close read.

Engaging in an exploratory approach toward implementing the Common Core does not replace or remove the need for long-term planning, such as curriculum maps, unit plans, and the like. That said, it makes little sense to ask teachers to simply plan entire units of aligned instruction and then go implement all of it when they may have had little-to-no experience thinking about and enacting purposeful standards-based instruction. Teachers already have plenty of experience planning; what they don't get practice with is expanding their practitioner knowledge in the context of the uncertain and complex situations of day-to-day teaching. That is what the inquiry approach provides and leverages.

Next Steps: Leading Learning

Your school's instructional leadership team or teacher collaboration teams can get started by taking the following steps.

- **Conduct an audit of your existing resources and needs:** What has been done already, what needs to be done, and where should you get started? Useful points for discussion include whether or not teachers have unwrapped or prioritized standards, selected a targeted instructional focus for their team, identified complex texts, and are collaborating on literacy instruction, and so on.

- **Set up a demonstration classroom:** Emphasizing practice in teacher learning means that sites of learning, such as classrooms, should be available for learning. Select classrooms to be open for colleagues to drop in and observe. Set a schedule and structure for conducting those observations.

○ **Pilot:** Have your instructional leadership team or a strong course or content team try out the inquiry cycle, monitoring progress and discussing how to adapt it for your school and teachers. Be sure to record the collaboration, or allow nonparticipating teachers to drop in and observe, so that the rest of the faculty can study the efforts when your school is ready to implement the approach on a wider scale.

○ **Develop a professional learning plan:** A professional learning plan typically is a six- to ten-week plan for focused staff development on a particular standard, problem of practice, or instructional goal (or two), complete with a calendar and a deliberate sequence of learning to ensure independent proficiency with the focus area. If your school or team has never created a long-term professional learning plan before, identify a modest objective or problem of practice your first time through and focus your collaboration on teacher experience and meaning making, such as through classroom observation and teacher reflection.

○ **Create text staircases:** Chapter 3 describes a process for creating long-term literacy plans. The sooner teams at your school have identified the complex texts needed for their respective courses, the easier it will be to create professional development plans and engage in an inquiry cycle to build teacher capacity to teach these texts effectively.

Effective teachers learn from and through practice, by testing out new texts and tasks, attending carefully to students' ideas, writing and discussing, and by inviting colleagues and peers into the classroom to observe and assist. And they talk about teaching—*their* teaching. The knowledge base needed for ambitious teaching exists within the walls of your school. Seek your answers there by doing the following.

Keep the Text at the Center

To become expert practitioners of literacy instruction, you need to be engaging expertly in the practice of literacy. To do so, focus collaborative time on reading and discussing the texts you are currently or may be teaching. You and your colleagues should look at the text as readers and as teachers to understand how the text works, how students might work through it, and how you might work to support students' work. This thorough analysis of the text accomplishes the same goals as collaborative instructional planning, while also deepening your collective content and implementation knowledge. This should be done frequently, such as on a weekly basis. It's among the most important work you can do.

Focus on Student Thinking

Supporting students as they engage complex texts demands a keen understanding of what students do and do not understand and how to respond instructionally to that comprehension (or lack thereof). It follows, then, that a critical part of teacher collaboration time should attend to and plan for students' thinking. Observe one another's classrooms, concentrating your observations and discussions on what students are doing. Review and assess student work. Plan for instruction by identifying the literacy demands of the chosen texts, likely student comprehension concerns, and the necessary supports to address these concerns. Most important, work together to position yourselves as listeners, using reading, writing, and thinking activities as opportunities for students to practice their ideas before being formally assessed on them.

Gain Expertise Through Enactment

The typical response by teachers and schools to the challenge of next-generation standards has been to focus on developing instructional plans, an understandable move given that unit plans are clear and finite products that can be created outside of the classroom. But making program shifts to incorporate, say, more close reading into the curriculum, does not account for the complex work of enacting and sustaining student interest in the work. The real shift of next-generation standards and assessments for teachers, it turns out, is what takes place *in* the classroom. This cannot be captured in a guide or a workshop; it has to be experienced in ways that are instructive to instruction. Make your classroom the setting for professional development and your teaching the professional development content. Leverage the combined talents of your community to plan, pilot, and process teaching together.

References and Resources

Achebe, C. (1959). *Things fall apart*. New York: McDowell, Obolensky.

Achebe, C. (2009). *The education of a British-protected child*. New York: Knopf.

Achieve the Core. (n.d.). *Updated text complexity grade bands and associated ranges from multiple measures*. Accessed at http://achievethecore.org/file/203 on March 6, 2015.

Achieve the Core. (2013). *Finding CCSS grade levels for texts: SCASS rubrics*. Accessed at http://achievethecore.org/page/656/finding-ccss-grade-levels-for-texts-scass -rubrics-list-pg on March 6, 2015.

ACT. (2006). *Reading between the lines: What the ACT reveals about college readiness in reading*. Iowa City, IA: Author. Accessed at www.act.org/research/policymakers/pdf /reading_summary.pdf on March 6, 2015.

Adichie, C. N. (2003). *Purple hibiscus*. Chapel Hill, NC: Algonquin Books of Chapel Hill.

Adichie, C. N. (2013). *Americanah*. New York: Knopf.

Adler, M. J., & Van Doren, C. (1972). *How to read a book: The classic guide to intelligent reading* (Rev. ed.). New York: Simon & Schuster.

Afflerbach, P., & Cho, B.-Y. (2009). Identifying and describing constructively responsive comprehension strategies in new and traditional forms of reading. In S. E. Israel & G. G. Duffy (Eds.), *Handbook of research on reading comprehension* (pp. 69–90). New York: Routledge.

Alston, C. L., & Barker, L. M. (2014). Reading for teaching: What we notice when we look at literature. *English Journal, 103*(4), 62–67.

Applebee, A. N., Langer, J. A., Nystrand, M., & Gamoran, A. (2003). Discussion-based approaches to developing understanding: Classroom instruction and student performance in middle and high school English. *American Educational Research Journal, 40*(3), 685–730.

Bain, R. B. (2005). "They thought the world was flat?" Applying the principles of *How People Learn* in teaching high school history. In M. S. Donovan & J. D. Bransford (Eds.), *How students learn: History in the classroom* (pp. 179–214). Washington, DC: National Academies Press.

Bain, R. B. (2012). Using disciplinary literacy to develop coherence in history teacher education: The clinical rounds project. *The History Teacher, 45*(4), 513–532.

Barringer, F. (2012, October 13). A grand experiment to rein in climate change. *New York Times.* Accessed at www.nytimes.com/2012/10/14/science/earth/in-california-a-grand-experiment-to-rein-in-climate-change.html?_r=0 on March 6, 2015.

Beck, I. L., & McKeown, M. G. (2006). *Improving comprehension with questioning the author: A fresh and expanded view of a powerful approach.* New York: Scholastic.

Beck, I. L., McKeown, M. G., Hamilton, R. L., & Kucan, L. (1997). *Questioning the author: An approach for enhancing student engagement with text.* Newark, DE: International Reading Association.

Beck, I. L., McKeown, M. G., Hamilton, R. L., & Kucan, L. (1998). Getting at the meaning: How to help students unpack difficult text. *American Educator, 22*(1–2), 66–71.

Beers, K., & Probst, R. E. (2013). *Notice and note: Strategies for close reading.* Portsmouth, NH: Heinemann.

Belenky, M. F., Clinchy, B. M., Goldberger, N. R., & Tarule, J. M. (1997). *Women's ways of knowing: The development of self, voice, and mind* (10th anniversary ed.). New York: Basic Books.

Berthoff, A. E. (1999). Reclaiming the active mind. *College English, 61*(6), 671–680.

Bloom, B. S. (1956). *Taxonomy of educational objectives, handbook I: The cognitive domain.* New York: David McKay.

Borko, H., Jacobs, J., & Koellner, K. (2010). Contemporary approaches to teacher professional development. In P. Peterson, E. Baker, & B. McGaw (Eds.), *International encyclopedia of education* (3rd ed., Vol. 7, pp. 548–556). Oxford, England: Elsevier.

Brookfield, S. D., & Preskill, S. (2005). *Discussion as a way of teaching: Tools and techniques for democratic classrooms* (2nd ed.). San Francisco: Jossey-Bass.

Bybee, R. W. (1997). *Achieving scientific literacy: From purposes to practices.* Portsmouth, NH: Heinemann.

Cain, K., Oakhill, J. V., Barnes, M. A., & Bryant, P. E. (2001). Comprehension skill, inference-making ability, and their relation to knowledge. *Memory and Cognition, 29*(6), 850–859.

Cartmill, E. A., Armstrong, B. F., Gleitman, L. R., Goldin-Meadow, S., Medina, T. N., & Trueswell, J. C. (2013). Quality of early parent input predicts child vocabulary 3 years later. *Proceedings of the National Academy of Sciences, 110*(28), 11278–11283.

Cazden, C. B. (2001). *Classroom discourse: The language of teaching and learning* (2nd ed.). Portsmouth, NH: Heinemann.

Chall, J. S. (1983). *Stages of reading development.* New York: McGraw-Hill.

Chall, J. S., Bissex, G. L., Conard, S. S., & Harris-Sharples, S. (1996). *Qualitative assessment of text difficulty: A practical guide for teachers and writers.* Cambridge, MA: Brookline Books.

Chinn, C. A., Anderson, R. C., & Waggoner, M. A. (2001). Patterns of discourse in two kinds of literature discussion. *Reading Research Quarterly, 36*(4), 378–411.

City, E. A., Elmore, R. F., Fiarman, S. E., & Teitel, L. (2009). *Instructional rounds in education: A network approach to improving teaching and learning.* Cambridge, MA: Harvard Education Press.

Clary, D. M., Styslinger, M. E., & Oglan, V. A. (2012). Literacy learning communities in partnership. *School–University Partnerships, 5*(1), 28–39.

Clifton, L. (2012). Won't you celebrate with me. In K. Young & M. Glazer (Eds.), *Collected poems of Lucille Clifton.* New York: BOA Editions.

Coleman, D., & Pimentel, S. (2012). *Revised publishers' criteria for the Common Core State Standards in English language arts and literacy, grades 3–12.* Accessed at www.corestandards.org/assets/Publishers_Criteria_for_3-12.pdf on March 6, 2015.

Collins, A., Brown, J. S., & Newman, S. E. (1989). Cognitive apprenticeship: Teaching the craft of reading, writing, and mathematics. In L. B. Resnick (Ed.), *Cognition and instruction: Issues and agendas* (pp. 453–494). Hillsdale, NJ: Erlbaum.

Collins, W., Colman, R., Haywood, J., Manning, M. R., & Mote, P. (2007). The physical science behind climate change. *Scientific American, 297*(2), 64–73.

Correnti, R., Matsumura, L. C., Hamilton, L., & Wang, E. (2013). Assessing students' skills at writing analytically in response to texts. *The Elementary School Journal, 114*(2), 142–177.

Danielson, C. (2011). *Enhancing professional practice: A framework for teaching.* Alexandria, VA: Association for Supervision and Curriculum Development.

Desimone, L. M. (2011). A primer on effective professional development. *Phi Delta Kappan, 92*(6), 68–71.

Dewey, J. (1935). *Liberalism and social action.* New York: Putnam.

Diamond, J. (1997). *Guns, germs, and steel: The fates of human societies.* New York: Norton.

Diamond, J. (2005). *Collapse: How societies choose to fail or succeed.* New York: Penguin.

Doctorow, E. L. (1975). *Ragtime.* New York: Random House.

Doyle, W. (1988). Work in mathematics classes: The context of students' thinking during instruction. *Educational Psychologist, 23*(2), 167–180.

Duke, N. K., & Pearson, P. D. (2002). Effective practices for developing reading comprehension: In A. E. Farstrup & S. J. Samuels (Eds.), *What research has to say about reading instruction* (3rd ed., pp. 205–242). Newark, DE: International Reading Association.

Dwyer, C. P., Hogan, M. J., & Stewart, I. (2013). An examination of the effects of argument mapping on students' memory and comprehension performance. *Thinking Skills and Creativity, 8,* 11–24.

Eckert, L. S. (2008). Bridging the pedagogical gap: Intersections between literary and reading theories in secondary and postsecondary literacy instruction. *Journal of Adolescent and Adult Literacy, 52*(2), 110–118.

Education Week Research Center. (2014). *From adoption to practice: Teacher perspectives on the Common Core.* Bethesda, MD: Author. Accessed at www.edweek.org/media /ewrc_teacherscommoncore_2014.pdf on March 9, 2015.

Ellison, R. (1952). *Invisible man.* New York: Random House.

Ericsson, K. A. (2002). Attaining excellence through deliberate practice: Insights from the study of expert performance. In M. Ferrari (Ed.), *The pursuit of excellence through education* (pp. 21–55). Mahwah, NJ: Erlbaum.

Erikson, E. H. (1968). *Identity: Youth and crisis.* New York: Norton.

Fennema, E., Carpenter, T. P., Franke, M. L., Levi, L., Jacobs, V. R., & Empson, S. B. (1996). A longitudinal study of learning to use children's thinking in mathematics instruction. *Journal for Research in Mathematics Education, 27*(4), 403–434.

Fernandez, C., & Yoshida, M. (2004). *Lesson study: A Japanese approach to improving mathematics teaching and learning.* Mahwah, NJ: Erlbaum.

Finkelstein, N. G., & Birn, R. B. (1998). *A nation on trial: The Goldhagen thesis and historical truth.* New York: Metropolitan Books.

Fisher, D., & Frey, N. (2008). *Better learning through structured teaching: A framework for the gradual release of responsibility.* Alexandria, VA: Association for Supervision and Curriculum Development.

Fisher, D., Frey, N., & Lapp, D. (2012). *Text complexity: Raising rigor in reading.* Newark, DE: International Reading Association.

Fitzgerald, F. S. (1925). *The great Gatsby.* New York: Scribner.

Foley, J. (2010). *The other inconvenient truth* [Video]. Accessed at www.ted.com/talks /jonathan_foley_the_other_inconvenient_truth?language=en on August 1, 2015.

Frager, A. M., & Frye, E. A. (2010). Focus on the essentials of reading instruction. *Phi Delta Kappan, 92*(2), 56–58.

Freebody, P., & Luke, A. (1990). 'Literacies' programs: Debates and demands in cultural context. *Prospect: An Australian Journal of TESOL, 5*(3), 7–16.

Frey, N., & Fisher, D. (2013). *Rigorous reading: 5 access points for comprehending complex texts.* Thousand Oaks, CA: Corwin Press.

Fukuyama, F. (1992). *The end of history and the last man.* New York: Free Press.

Gladwell, M. (2002). The talent myth: Are smart people overrated? *The New Yorker, 78,* 28–33.

Glazer, E. M., & Hannafin, M. J. (2006). The collaborative apprenticeship model: Situated professional development within school settings. *Teaching and Teacher Education, 22*(2), 179–193.

Goldman, S. R. (2012). Adolescent literacy: Learning and understanding content. *Future of Children, 22*(2), 89–116.

Goldman, S. R., & Lee, C. D. (2014). Text complexity: State of the art and the conundrums it raises. *The Elementary School Journal, 115*(2), 290–300.

Gomez, L. M., & Gomez, K. (2007). Reading for learning: Literacy supports for 21st-century work. *Phi Delta Kappan, 89*(3), 224–228.

Graesser, A. C., McNamara, D. S., Louwerse, M. M., & Cai, Z. (2004). Coh-Metrix: Analysis of text on cohesion and language. *Behavior Research Methods, Instruments, and Computers, 36*(2), 193–202.

Gregory, J. N. (2005). *The southern diaspora: How the great migrations of black and white southerners transformed America.* Chapel Hill: University of North Carolina Press.

Grossman, P., Wineburg, S., & Woolworth, S. (2001). Toward a theory of teacher community. *Teachers College Record, 103*(6), 942–1012.

Grouws, D. A., & Cebulla, K. J. (2000). *Improving student achievement in mathematics* (Educational Practices Series—4). Brussels, Belgium: International Academy of Education.

Guthrie, J. T., Wigfield, A., Barbosa, P., Perencevich, K. C., Taboada, A., Davis, M. H., et al. (2004). Increasing reading comprehension and engagement through concept-oriented reading instruction. *Journal of Educational Psychology, 96*(3), 403–423.

Habermas, J. (1990). *Moral consciousness and communicative action* (C. Lenhardt & S. W. Nicholsen, Trans.). Cambridge: Massachusetts Institute of Technology Press. (Original work published 1983)

Hargreaves, A. (2003). *Teaching in the knowledge society: Education in the age of insecurity.* New York: Teachers College Press.

Hegarty, M. (2005). Multimedia learning about physical systems. In R. E. Mayer (Ed.), *The Cambridge handbook of multimedia learning* (pp. 447–465). New York: Cambridge University Press.

Henderson, M. B., Peterson, P. E., & West, M. R. (2015). No common opinion on the Common Core. *Education Next, 15*(1), 9–19.

Herman, J., & Linn, R. (2014). New assessments, new rigor. *Educational Leadership, 71*(6), 34–37.

Hertzog, H. S. (2002). When, how, and who do I ask for help? Novices' perceptions of problems and assistance. *Teacher Education Quarterly, 29*(3), 25–41.

Hess, K., & Biggam, S. (2004). *A discussion of "increasing text complexity."* Dover, NH: National Center for the Improvement of Educational Assessment. Accessed at www .nciea.org/publications/TextComplexity_KH05.pdf on March 9, 2015.

Hiebert, E. H. (2012). *The text complexity multi-index.* Santa Cruz, CA: TextProject.

Hiebert, E. H., & Grisham, D. L. (2013). What literacy teacher educators need to know about supporting teachers in understanding text complexity within the Common Core State Standards. *Journal of Reading Education, 37*(3), 5–12.

Hiebert, J., & Morris, A. K. (2012). Teaching, rather than teachers, as a path toward improving classroom instruction. *Journal of Teacher Education, 63*(2), 92–102.

Homer. (1996). *The odyssey* (R. Fagles, Trans.). New York: Penguin.

Intergovernmental Panel on Climate Change. (2013). *Climate change 2013: The physical science basis.* New York: Cambridge University Press. Accessed at www.ipcc.ch/pdf /assessment-report/ar5/wg1/WG1AR5_ALL_FINAL.pdf on March 12, 2015.

Jaeger, C. C., Hasselmann, K., Leipold, G., Mangalagiu, D., & Tabara, J. D. (Eds.). (2012). *Reframing the problem of climate change: From zero sum game to win-win solutions.* New York: Earthscan.

Kane, G. (2005). The mysteries of mass. *Scientific American, 293*(1), 40–48.

King, M. L. K., Jr. (1963). *I have a dream.* Accessed at www.archives.gov/press/exhibits /dream-speech.pdf on June 26, 2015.

Kosanovich, M. L., Reed, D. K., & Miller, D. H. (2010). *Bringing literacy strategies into content instruction: Professional learning for secondary-level teachers.* Portsmouth, NH: Center on Instruction, RMC Research.

Kucan, L., & Palincsar, A. S. (2011). Locating struggling readers in a reconfigured landscape: A conceptual review. In M. L. Kamil, P. D. Pearson, E. B. Moje, & P. P. Afflerbach (Eds.), *Handbook of reading research* (Vol. 4, pp. 341–358). New York: Routledge.

Kurtz, K. J., Boukrina, O., & Gentner, D. (2013). Comparison promotes learning and transfer of relational categories. *Journal of Experimental Psychology: Learning, Memory, and Cognition, 39*(4), 1303–1310.

Lampert, M., Franke, M. L., Kazemi, E., Ghousseini, H., Turrou, A. C., Beasley, H., et al. (2013). Keeping it complex: Using rehearsals to support novice teacher learning of ambitious teaching. *Journal of Teacher Education, 64*(3), 226–243.

Lampert, M., & Graziani, F. (2009). Instructional activities as a tool for teachers' and teacher educators' learning. *The Elementary School Journal, 109*(5), 491–509.

Langer, J. A. (1994). A response-based approach to reading literature. *Language Arts, 71*(3), 203–211.

Lawrence, J., & Bunch, L. G. (1993). *Jacob Lawrence: The migration series.* Urbana, VA: Rappahannock Press.

Lee, C. D. (2001). Is October Brown Chinese? A cultural modeling activity system for underachieving students. *American Educational Research Journal, 38*(1), 97–141.

Lee, C. D. (2007). *Culture, literacy, and learning: Blooming in the midst of the whirlwind.* New York: Teachers College Press.

Lee, H. (1960). *To kill a mockingbird.* Philadelphia: Lippincott.

Lent, R. C. (2007). *Literacy learning communities: A guide for creating sustainable change in secondary schools.* Portsmouth, NH: Heinemann.

Lewis, C. C. (2002). *Lesson study: A handbook of teacher-led instructional change.* Philadelphia: Research for Better Schools.

Liben, D., & Pearson, P. D. (2013). *The progression of reading comprehension.* Accessed at http://achievethecore.org/content/upload/liben_pearson_progression_of _comprehension_research_ela.pdf on March 9, 2015.

Litman, C., Marple, S., Greenleaf, C., Charney-Sirott, I., Bolz, M., Richardson, L., et al. (2014). *Argumentation opportunity to learn in secondary English language arts, history, and science classrooms.* Accessed at https://secure.literacyresearchassociation .org/papers/lra20141119134324.pdf on March 9, 2015.

Lounsberry, B. (1990). *The art of fact.* Santa Barbara, CA: Praeger.

Magliano, J. P., Millis, K., Ozuru, Y., & McNamara, D. S. (2007). A multidimensional framework to evaluate reading assessment tools. In D. S. McNamara (Ed.), *Reading comprehension strategies: Theories, interventions, and technologies* (pp. 107–136). Mahwah, NJ: Erlbaum.

Marzano, R. J. (2004). *Building background knowledge for academic achievement: Research on what works in schools.* Alexandria, VA: Association for Supervision and Curriculum Development.

Mason, Z. (2007). *The lost books of* The Odyssey. Buffalo, NY: Starcherone Books.

Mathis, A. (2013). *The twelve tribes of Hattie.* New York: Vintage Books.

Matthews, P., & Rittle-Johnson, B. (2009). In pursuit of knowledge: Comparing self-explanations, concepts, and procedures as pedagogical tools. *Journal of Experimental Child Psychology, 104*(1), 1–21.

McCarthy, C. (1985). *Blood meridian: Or the evening redness in the West.* New York: Random House.

McDonald, M., Kazemi, E., & Kavanagh, S. S. (2013). Core practices and pedagogies of teacher education: A call for a common language and collective activity. *Journal of Teacher Education, 64*(5), 378–386.

McLaughlin, M., & DeVoogd, G. (2004). *Critical literacy: Enhancing students' comprehension of text.* New York: Scholastic.

Mendel, G. (1865). *Experiments in plant hybridization.* Accessed at www.mendelweb .org/Mendel.html on June 26, 2015.

Mercer, N. (2002). Developing dialogues. In G. Wells & G. Claxton (Eds.), *Learning for life in the 21st century: Sociocultural perspectives on the future of education* (pp. 141–153). Malden, MA: Blackwell.

Mercer, N., Wegerif, R., & Dawes, L. (1999). Children's talk and the development of reasoning in the classroom. *British Educational Research Journal, 25*(1), 95–111.

Michaels, S., O'Connor, M. C., Hall, M. W., & Resnick, L. B. (2010). *Accountable Talk sourcebook: For classroom conversation that works.* Pittsburgh, PA: University of Pittsburgh Institute for Learning.

Michaels, S., O'Connor, C., & Resnick, L. B. (2008). Deliberative discourse idealized and realized: Accountable talk in the classroom and in civic life. *Studies in Philosophy and Education, 27*(4), 283–297.

Michaels, S., Sohmer, R., & O'Connor, M. C. (2006). Discourse in the classroom. In H. E. Wiegand (Ed.), *Sociolinguistics: An international handbook of the science of language and society* (pp. 2351–2366). New York: de Gruyter.

Mikics, D. (2007). *A new handbook of literary terms.* New Haven, CT: Yale University Press.

Milner, J. O., & Milner, L. F. M. (2003). *Bridging English* (3rd ed.). Upper Saddle River, NJ: Prentice Hall.

Monte-Sano, C. (2011). Beyond reading comprehension and summary: Learning to read and write in history by focusing on evidence, perspective, and interpretation. *Curriculum Inquiry, 41*(2), 212–249.

Morsy, L., Kieffer, M., & Snow, C. (2010). *Measure for measure: A critical consumers' guide to reading comprehension assessments for adolescents.* New York: Carnegie.

Murphy, P. K., Wilkinson, I. A. G., Soter, A. O., Hennessey, M. N., & Alexander, J. F. (2009). Examining the effects of classroom discussion on students' comprehension of text: A meta-analysis. *Journal of Educational Psychology, 101*(3), 740–764.

National Commission on Writing in America's Schools and Colleges. (2003). *The neglected "R": The need for a writing revolution.* New York: College Entrance Examination Board.

National Governors Association Center for Best Practices & Council of Chief State School Officers. (n.d.a). *Common Core State Standards for English language arts & literacy in history/social studies, science, and technical subjects: Appendix A—Research supporting key elements of the standards.* Washington, DC: Author. Accessed at www .corestandards.org/assets/Appendix_A.pdf on March 10, 2015.

National Governors Association Center for Best Practices & Council of Chief State School Officers. (n.d.b). *Common Core State Standards for English language arts & literacy in history/social studies, science, and technical subjects: Appendix B—Text exemplars and sample performance tasks.* Washington, DC: Author. Accessed at www .corestandards.org/assets/Appendix_B.pdf on March 10, 2015.

National Governors Association Center for Best Practices & Council of Chief State School Officers. (n.d.c). *Common Core State Standards for English language arts & literacy in history/social studies, science, and technical subjects: Appendix C—Samples of student writing.* Washington, DC: Author. Accessed at www.corestandards.org /assets/Appendix_C.pdf on March 10, 2015.

National Governors Association Center for Best Practices & Council of Chief State School Officers. (2010). *Common Core State Standards for English language arts and literacy in history/social studies, science, and technical subjects.* Washington, DC: Authors. Accessed at www.corestandards.org/assets/CCSSI_ELA%20Standards.pdf on March 10, 2015.

National Reading Panel. (2000). *Teaching children to read: An evidence-based assessment of the scientific research literature on reading and its implications for reading instruction* (NIH Publication No. 00-4769). Washington, DC: U.S. Government Printing Office.

Nelson, J., Perfetti, C., Liben, D., & Liben, M. (2012). *Measures of text difficulty: Testing their predictive value for grade levels and student performance.* New York: Student Achievement Partners.

Nokes, J. D., Dole, J. A., & Hacker, D. J. (2007). Teaching high school students to use heuristics while reading historical texts. *Journal of Educational Psychology, 99*(3), 492–504.

Nystrand, M. (1997). *Opening dialogue: Understanding the dynamics of language and learning in the English classroom.* New York: Teachers College Press.

O'Sullivan, J. (1839). *The great nation of futurity.* Accessed at http://web.utk.edu /~mfitzge1/docs/374/GNF1839.pdf on June 26, 2015.

Orlando, V. P., Caverly, D. C., Swetnam, L., & Flippo, R. F. (1989). Text demands in college classes: An investigation. *Forum for Reading, 21*(1), 43–48.

Palincsar, A. S., & Brown, A. L. (1984). Reciprocal teaching of comprehension-fostering and comprehension-monitoring activities. *Cognition and Instruction, 1*(2), 117–175.

Palincsar, A. S., & Magnusson, S. J. (2001). The interplay of first-hand and second-hand investigations to model and support the development of scientific knowledge and reasoning. In S. M. Carver & D. Klahr (Eds.), *Cognition and instruction: Twenty-five years of progress* (pp. 151–193). Mahwah, NJ: Erlbaum.

Paul, R., & Elder, L. (2006). *Critical thinking: Learn the tools the best thinkers use* (Concise ed.). New York: Pearson/Prentice Hall.

Perry, W. G., Jr. (1999). *Forms of intellectual and ethical development in the college years: A scheme.* San Francisco: Jossey-Bass.

Piercy, T., & Piercy, W. (2011). *Disciplinary literacy: Redefining deep understanding and leadership for 21st-century demands.* Englewood, CO: Lead + Learn Press.

Porter-O'Donnell, C. (2004). Beyond the yellow highlighter: Teaching annotation skills to improve reading comprehension. *English Journal, 93*(5), 82–89.

Probst, R. E. (1988). Dialogue with a text. *English Journal, 77*(1), 32–38.

Reisman, A. (2012). The "document-based lesson": Bringing disciplinary inquiry into high school history classrooms with adolescent struggling readers. *Journal of Curriculum Studies, 44*(2), 233–264.

Resnick, L. B. (1987). *Education and learning to think.* Washington, DC: National Academies Press.

Resnick, L. B., Michaels, S., & O'Connor, C. (2010). How (well-structured) talk builds the mind. In R. J. Sternberg & D. D. Preiss (Eds.), *From genes to context: New discoveries about learning from educational research and their applications* (pp. 163–194). New York: Springer.

Resnick, L. B., O'Connor, C., & Michaels, S. (2007). *Classroom discourse, mathematical rigor, and student reasoning: An accountable talk literature review.* Pittsburgh, PA: LearnLab, Pittsburgh Science of Learning Center.

Rosenblatt, L. M. (1994). *The reader, the text, the poem: The transactional theory of the literary work.* Carbondale: Southern Illinois University Press.

Roy, M., & Chi, M. T. H. (2005). The self-explanation principle in multimedia learning. In R. E. Mayer (Ed.), *Cambridge handbook of multimedia learning* (pp. 271–286). New York: Cambridge University Press.

Sachs, S. (2000, January 9). American dream, no illusions; immigrant literature now about more than fitting in. *New York Times.* Accessed at www.nytimes.com /2000/01/09/nyregion/american-dream-no-illusions-immigrant-literature-now -about-more-than-fitting-in.html on March 6, 2015.

Schlesinger, A. M., Jr. (1986). *The cycles of American history.* Boston: Houghton Mifflin.

Schwarz, B. B., & Asterhan, C. S. C. (2010). Argumentation and reasoning. In K. Littleton, C. Wood, & J. K. Staarman (Eds.), *International handbook of psychology in education* (pp. 137–176). Bingley, England: Emerald Group.

Seixas, P. (2008). *"Scaling up" the benchmarks of historical thinking: A report on the Vancouver meetings, February 14–15, 2008.* Vancouver, British Columbia, Canada: Centre for the Study of Historical Consciousness, University of British Columbia. Accessed at http://historicalthinking.ca/sites/default/files/files/docs/Scaling% 20Up%20Meeting%20Report.pdf on March 9, 2015.

Sfard, A. (1998). On two metaphors for learning and the dangers of choosing just one. *Educational Researcher, 27*(2), 4–13.

Sfard, A., & Kieran, C. (2001). Cognition as communication: Rethinking learning-by-talking through multi-faceted analysis of students' mathematical interactions. *Mind, Culture, and Activity, 8*(1), 42–76.

Shakespeare, W. (1992). *Romeo and Juliet* (B. A. Mowat & P. Werstine, Eds.). New York: Washington Square Press.

Shanahan, T., Callison, K., Carriere, C., Duke, N. K., Pearson, P. D., Schatschneider, C., et al. (2010). *Improving reading comprehension in kindergarten through 3rd grade: IES practice guide* (NCEE 2010-4038). Washington, DC: National Center for Education Evaluation and Regional Assistance, Institute of Education Sciences, U.S. Department of Education. Accessed at http://ies.ed.gov/ncee/wwc/pdf /practice_guides/readingcomp_pg_092810.pdf on March 9, 2015.

Shanahan, T., & Duffett, A. (2013). *Common Core in the schools: A first look at reading assignments*. Washington, DC: Thomas B. Fordham Institute.

Sheehan, K. M., Kostin, I., Napolitano, D., & Flor, M. (2014). The TextEvaluator tool: Helping teachers and test developers select texts for use in instruction and assessment. *The Elementary School Journal, 115*(2), 184–209.

Simpson, M. L., Stahl, N. A., & Francis, M. A. (2004). Reading and learning strategies: Recommendations for the 21st century. *Journal of Developmental Education, 28*(2), 2–15.

Skloot, R. (2010). *The immortal life of Henrietta Lacks*. New York: Crown.

Smith, H. N. (1970). *Virgin land: The American West as symbol and myth*. Cambridge, MA: Harvard University Press.

Soter, A. O., Wilkinson, I. A., Murphy, P. K., Rudge, L., Reninger, K., & Edwards, M. (2008). What the discourse tells us: Talk and indicators of high-level comprehension. *International Journal of Educational Research, 47*(6), 372–391.

Staples, B. (1986, September). Just walk on by: A Black man ponders his power to alter public space. *Ms. Magazine*.

Stein, M. K., & Smith, M. S. (1998). Mathematical tasks as a framework for reflection: From research to practice. *Mathematics Teaching in the Middle School, 3*(4), 268–275.

Stephanson, A. (1995). *Manifest destiny: American expansion and the empire of right*. New York: HarperCollins.

Sweller, J. (2010). Cognitive load theory: Recent theoretical advances. In J. L. Plass, R. Moreno, & R. Brünken (Eds.), *Cognitive load theory* (pp. 29–47). New York: Cambridge University Press.

Taboada, A., & Guthrie, J. T. (2006). Contributions of student questioning and prior knowledge to construction of knowledge from reading information text. *Journal of Literacy Research, 38*(1), 1–35.

Tyson, N. D. (1996). In defense of the Big Bang. *Natural History, 105*(12), 76.

Valencia, S. W., Wixson, K. K., & Pearson, P. D. (2014). Putting text complexity in context: Refocusing on comprehension of complex text. *Elementary School Journal, 115*(2), 270–289.

van Gelder, T. (2003). Enhancing deliberation through computer supported argument visualization. In P. A. Kirschner, S. J. B. Shum, & C. S. Carr (Eds.), *Visualizing argumentation: Software tools for collaborative and educational sense-making* (pp. 97–115). New York: Springer.

Vogler, C. (2007). *The writer's journey: Mythic structure for writers* (3rd ed.). Studio City, CA: Wiese.

Wade, S., Thompson, A., & Watkins, W. (1994). The role of belief systems in authors' and readers' constructions of texts. In R. Garner & P. A. Alexander (Eds.), *Beliefs about text and instruction with text* (pp. 265–293). Hillsdale, NJ: Erlbaum.

Wainaina, B. (2011). *One day I will write about this place: A memoir.* Minneapolis, MN: Graywolf Press.

Walzer, M. (1990). What does it mean to be an "American"? *Social Research, 57*(3), 591–614.

Washington Times. (1916, October 23). South unable to put a stop to the Negro exodus. Accessed at http://chroniclingamerica.loc.gov/lccn/sn84026749/1916-10-23/ed-1/seq-1/ on November 11, 2014.

Webb, N. L. (2002). *Alignment study in language arts, mathematics, science, and social studies of state standards and assessments for four states.* Washington, DC: Council of Chief State School Officers.

Wells, G. (1994). The complementary contributions of Halliday and Vygotsky to a "language-based theory of learning." *Linguistics and Education, 6*(1), 41–90.

White, S. (2012). Mining the text: 34 text features that can ease or obstruct text comprehension and use. *Literacy Research and Instruction, 51*(2), 143–164.

Wiggins, G. P., & McTighe, J. (2005). *Understanding by design.* Alexandria, VA: Association for Supervision and Curriculum Development.

Wiley, J., & Voss, J. F. (1999). Constructing arguments from multiple sources: Tasks that promote understanding and not just memory for text. *Journal of Educational Psychology, 91*(2), 301–311.

Wilkerson, I. (2010). *The warmth of other suns: The epic story of America's great migration.* New York: Random House.

Wilkinson, I. A. G., Soter, A. O., & Murphy, P. K. (2010). Developing a model of quality talk about literary text. In M. G. McKeown & L. Kucan (Eds.), *Bringing reading research to life* (pp. 142–169). New York: Guilford Press.

Williamson, G. L. (2008). A text readability continuum for postsecondary readiness. *Journal of Advanced Academics, 19*(4), 602–632.

Williamson, G. L., Fitzgerald, J., & Stenner, J. A. (2014). Student reading growth illuminates the Common Core text-complexity standard: Raising both bars. *Elementary School Journal, 115*(2), 230–254.

Willingham, D. T. (2007). Critical thinking: Why is it so hard to teach? *American Educator.* Accessed at www.aft.org/sites/default/files/periodicals/Crit_Thinking.pdf on March 6, 2015.

Willingham, D. T. (2009). *Why don't students like school?: A cognitive scientist answers questions about how the mind works and what it means for the classroom.* San Francisco: Jossey-Bass.

Wilson, M. B. (2012). *Interactive modeling: A powerful technique for teaching children.* Turners Falls, MA: Northeast Foundation for Children.

Windschitl, M., Thompson, J., & Braaten, M. (2009, April). *Fostering ambitious pedagogy in novice teachers: The role of tool-supported analyses of student work.* Paper presented at the annual conference of the National Association of Research in Science Teaching, San Diego, CA.

Wineburg, S., & Martin, D. (2009). Tampering with history: Adapting primary sources for struggling readers. *Social Education, 73*(5), 212–216.

Wood, G. S. (1992). *The radicalism of the American Revolution.* New York: Knopf.

World Bank. (2012). *Turn down the heat: Why a 4°C warmer world must be avoided.* Accessed at www-wds.worldbank.org/external/default/WDSContentServer /WDSP/IB/2015/07/17/090224b0828c33e7/1_0/Rendered/PDF /Turn0down0the00orld0must0be0avoided.pdf on August 1, 2015.

X, M., & Haley, A. (1965). *The autobiography of Malcolm X: As told to Alex Haley.* New York: Grove Press.

Index

Using Technology to Enhance Writing
Edited by Richard E. Ferdig, Timothy V. Rasinski, and Kristine E. Pytash

Sharpen your students' communication skills while integrating digital tools into writing instruction. Loaded with techniques for planning and organizing writing, this handbook troubleshoots issues students face when writing in a printed versus digital context and teaches them how to read in multiple mediums.
BKF607

Using Technology to Enhance Reading
Edited by Timothy V. Rasinski, Kristine E. Pytash, and Richard E. Ferdig

Discover how technological resources can improve the effectiveness and breadth of reading instruction to build student knowledge. Read real-world accounts from literacy experts, and learn how their methods can be adapted for your classroom.
BKF608

Building a Common Core–Based Curriculum
Susan Udelhofen

Explore various stages of curriculum development, from the preliminary work of building academic support to creating curriculum maps and tracking improvement goals. Learn to effectively share information during the curriculum-building process, and engage in significant, collaborative conversations around the curriculum.
BKF549

Unstoppable Learning
Douglas Fisher and Nancy Frey

Discover how systems thinking can enhance teaching and learning schoolwide. Examine how to use systems thinking—which involves distinguishing patterns and considering short- and long-term consequences—to better understand the big picture of education and the intricate relationships that impact classrooms.
BKF662

> I came to the presentation pretty much devoid of an understanding of how the **Common Core** was going to affect my students and my instructional methods. I walked away **excited** and feeling **validated**.
>
> ## I'm on board!

—David Nohe, teacher,
New Mexico School for the Blind and Visually Impaired

 PD Services

Our experts draw from decades of research and their own experiences to bring you practical strategies for integrating the Common Core. You can choose from a range of customizable services, from a one-day overview to a multiyear process.

Book your CCSS PD today!
888.763.9045

Solution Tree